RP
9.99

Doing Resear

ROB WALKER

DOING RESEARCH

A handbook for
teachers

ROUTLEDGE

First published 1985 by Methuen & Co. Ltd
Reprinted 1986
Reprinted 1989, 1990, 1993
by Routledge
11 New Fetter Lane, London EC4P 4EE

© 1985 Rob Walker

Printed and bound in Great Britain by The University Press, Cambridge

British Library Cataloguing in Publication Data

Walker, Rob
Doing research.
1. Education−Research
I. Title
370′.7′8   LB1028
ISBN 0-415-03688-7 Pbk

Contents

Acknowledgements

My thanks to:

those students, academic and other staff, visitors and examiners who, over the years, have contributed to the teaching programme in CARE: it is on the basis of their experience that this book is written;

Jennifer Nias and her colleagues at the Cambridge Institute of Education;

Clem Adelman, for reading an early draft and offering critical comments;

the Education Department, York University, for sharing their thoughts on some of the concerns raised here;

John Henry, Stephen Rowlands, Helen Simons, Dave Ebbutt, Gordon Bell, Wilf Carr, Stephen Kemmis and others, whose work has made me realize that this book is far from complete;

John Jennings of Norwich Teachers' Centre, Chris Saville and Tony Andrews, who made much of what is reported here possible;

Lionel Hope Jones, copy editor and clear thinker;

Lynne Walker, for getting me started and encouraging me to continue.

I would also like to thank the following for permission to reproduce copyright material:

Clem Adelman for extracts from his two SSRC reports on *The*

Acknowledgements vii

Use of Objects in the Education of Children 3–5 Years (1976)
the American Educational Research Association for pp. 116–17
and 135–8 from R. E. Stake and C. Gjerde, 'An evaluation of
TCITY, the Twin City Institute for Talented Youth 1971',
from R. Kraft *et al.* (eds), *Four Evaluation Examples: Anthropological, Economic, Narrative and Portrayal*, Chicago, Rand
McNally College Publishing Co., 1974 (©1974 by American
Educational Research Association, Washington, DC)
the Australian Association for the Teaching of English, Inc., for
an extract from B. Beasley and L. Riordan, 'The classroom
teacher as researcher', *English in Australia*, No. 55 (1981)
the Cambridge Institute of Education for extracts from L.
Browning *et al.*, *Team Based Action Research* (n.d.); J. Elliott,
'Action Research into action research', *Classroom Action
Research Bulletin*, No. 5 (1982); K. Forsyth and J. Wood,
'Summary of classroom research techniques', from J. Elliott
and C. Adelman (eds), *Ways of Doing Research in Your Own
Classroom* (n.d.); D. Ireland and T. Russell, 'Pattern analysis as
used in the Ottawa Valley Teaching Project', *CARN Newsletter*
(1978); and for the figure on p. 197, from J. Elliott, *Action
Research: A Framework for Self Evaluation in Schools* (1981), p. 3
CARE, University of East Anglia, for extracts from B.
MacDonald and R. Stake, 'The first year of the National
Development Programme in Computer-Assisted Learning
from an issues perspective' (1974); and B. MacDonald and R.
Walker, *Information Evaluation Research and the Problem of Control*
(1974)
Deakin University for checklists from C. Hook, *Studying
Classrooms* (1981), pp. 81 and 82; and for the figure on p. 196,
from S. Kemmis *et al.*, *The Action Research Planner* (1982), p. 8
Dave Ebbutt for the figure on pp. 198–9, from 'Educational
Action Research: some general concerns and specific quibbles'
(1982)
Heinemann Educational Books, the author, and Watson, Little
Ltd, for an extract from E. Richardson, *The Teacher, the School
and the Task of Management* (1973)
David Higham Associates Ltd for an extract from Ronald
Blythe, *Akenfield* (1972)
the Director, Institute for Research in Teaching, College of
Education, University of Michigan, for extracts from F.

Erickson and J. Wilson, *Sights and Sounds of Life in Schools* (1982) the Oryx Press, 2214 N. Central Ave., Phoenix, Arizona 85004, for an extract from *Current Index to Journals in Education*, 14, 1 (1982)

the Managing Editor, *Personnel Psychology*, for the figure on p. 47, from V. R. Boehm, 'Research in the "Real World": a conceptual model', *Personnel Psychology*, 33 (1980), p. 496

Sage Publications, Inc. for an extract from R. Faulkner, 'Improvising on a triad', from J. van Maanen *et al.*, *Varieties of Qualitative Research* (1982); two tables from B. MacDonald and J. Sanger, 'Just for the record?: notes towards a theory of interviewing in evaluation', from E. House (ed.), *Evaluation Review Studies Annual*, 7 (1982); and a checklist from J Millman, 'A checklist procedure', from N. L. Smith (ed.), *New Techniques for Evaluation* (1981), pp. 316–18

R. E. Stake for extracts from his *Evaluating Educational Programmes: the Need and the Response* (1976) and from R. E. Stake and J. E. Easley, *Survey Findings* (1977)

Taylor & Francis Ltd for an extract from S. Kemmis and I. Robottom, 'Principles of procedure in curriculum evaluation', *Journal of Curriculum Studies*, 13, 2 (1981)

Teachers College Press for pp. 58–9 and 68–72 from Ann E. Boehm and Richard A. Weinberg, *The Classroom Observer: A Guide for Developing Observation Skills*, New York, Teachers College Press (© 1977 by Teachers College, Columbia University. All rights reserved)

Janine Wiedel for the photographs on p. 142.

1 Applied research and problems of course design

This book is written with a specific audience in mind – those teachers who attend (and run) courses which include an element of applied research, action research or evaluation, especially those involving a practical assignment or dissertation.

There is a need for such a book at the present time because of a recent expansion in the availability of such courses (especially of in-service courses leading to qualifications). This expansion may be seen as the next logical step in the evolution of a curriculum reform movement which has progressed from an emphasis on materials production to a stress on teacher development, and from central to local developments. It is in part a result of organizational initiatives (by the Open University, the CNAA and individual polytechnics, universities, colleges and institutes), spurred on by changes in their functions resulting from a series of contractions in the market for initially trained teachers. It is, too, in part a result of pressures for professional accountability and institutional responsiveness particularly at the local level.

Those of us who promote, teach and examine such courses tend to rely on each other for access to an appropriate literature. As often happens when new areas develop fast, an invisible college steps into gaps left by conventional publication. Students who have attended such courses will recognize the experience of being deluged by mimeographed papers, photocopies of photocopies, and even copies of handwritten drafts. One of the early 'classic' papers in the field, Parlett and Hamilton's statement of 'illuminative evaluation' (1972), having failed to find a journal publisher, was run off in an edition of some two hundred copies, yet within months had circulated underground in numerous forms in what must have been at least a tenfold multiple of the original print run.

Gradually books have appeared which have opened access to the underground literature. Hamilton *et al.*'s *Beyond The Numbers Game* (1977) sets out clearly the state of evaluation theory, though the number of empirical examples the editors were able to include at the time was limited. Lawrence Stenhouse's books on curriculum (1975, 1978 and 1983), though written in a deceptively easy style, set out the notion of curriculum research which provides an essential perspective. The Open University (and in Australia, Deakin University) have consistently made the ideas available in the form of course materials, in case studies and in book form.

A significant gap which remains is in the area of research methods and techniques. Generally the developments I have been talking about, which cross the areas of curriculum, evaluation and teacher education, have leant on the social science tradition of qualitative, interpretive research. Students are usually referred to the work of the Chicago School though the reference is somewhat narrow (that is to say, reference is made at the technical level to the uses made of interviews and observations, not to the notion of the sociology of occupations). Renewed interest in the Chicago School has also been a feature of British sociology in the last decade (and particularly in the sociology of education). The 'discovery', not just of symbolic interactionism but also of ethnomethodology, and a later structuralist reaction against them, have created a busy and productive (and almost exclusively British) research genre. (See, for example, Woods, 1979, 1980a, 1980b; Chanan and Delamont, 1975: Stubbs and Delamont, 1976; Hammersley, 1983; Hammersley and Atkinson, 1983; Woods and Hammersley, 1976; Delamont, 1983; Willis, 1977; Sharp and Green, 1975; and also the relevant Open University courses.) This body of research has run alongside the development of school-based curriculum and evaluation research which forms the focus for this book. Its concerns are more with social science than with educational practice but it provides a valuable body of empirical work, a series of useful points of reference and the ground for methodological debate.

This book addresses a small corner of the field, but one which is crucial. It provides access to research methods and techniques which might be used by teachers in the context of applied research, action research or evaluation. As such it does not require a prior background in social science (neither does it deny it!). It attempts to relate research techniques to the contexts in which they will be used, and as such is intended to be more than a research manual.

At present the texts available tend to be oriented to social science research (e.g. McCall and Simmons, 1969; Filstead, 1970; Schatzman and Strauss, 1973). They require a considerable social science background and they assume that the products of research will be of a social science kind rather than intended for educational use. Because they are written as technical sources and so assume a knowledgeable readership, there is a danger that, taken out of context, they result in a view of research methods and techniques as recipe knowledge. They are, therefore, not ideal texts, though valuable for their thoroughness and attention to detail. The reader needs to be aware that their concentration on questions of method and technique should not lead to a neglect of questions of need, intent and purpose.

This book is less thorough in its treatment of technical issues but attempts to set the applied research enterprise in a professional context. It is intended to be used in parallel to the standard methodological texts rather than to replace them, and to provide a series of signposts rather than prescriptions and procedures. In part this is because it takes a somewhat different view of 'research' from most conventional texts.

In writing this book I have taken the view that research is an essential element in the teacher's role. As teaching has become increasingly professionalized and the management of educational organizations more systematized, so 'research' has increasingly become something that teachers are expected to include in their repertoire of skills. By 'research' I do not mean detailed knowledge of the literature or high levels of proficiency in the skills conventionally required by testing and survey research. For one thing, to become expert in either of these areas demands more time, more training and more experience than most teachers are able to accumulate. What is required of teachers, of schools and of school systems is a range of other research skills, usually in relation to an immediate issue in one's own institution:

- the need to review a range of alternative curriculum proposals and to judge their likely impact in practice
- the need to evaluate practice, performance and policy in teaching and in administration
- the need to provide evidence and analysis of the school's programme for management purposes or to inform the LEA, school governors, parents and others
- the need to interpret and to assess information coming into schools from a variety of sources – from examination boards, from the LEA, from HMI, from the APU, from the academic world, etc.
- the need to make effective use of information provided by agencies that are concerned with pupils but do not necessarily share educational assumptions or use the language of schooling; e.g. the social services, the MSC, employers.

When most of us think about educational research we tend first to think about data collection, but the kinds of research skills in demand here are not only those of information collection. These concerns involve the full range of skills required to identify issues and problems, to assess different information sources, to collect further information or design further enquiries, to interpret information already available and to communicate improved understanding to those directly implicated.

A glance at most university and college libraries shows that the sections on research methods tend to be well stocked with books that take a narrower and more academic view. The assumption generally made is that research involves the collection of relatively purified data framed in relation to a theoretical problem that comes from the researcher. There is very little consideration of the 'messy' practical problems that arise in handling 'natural' information in relation to professional or practical issues or concerns.

Indeed it could be argued that there is very little *educational* research available – in the sense of disciplined research conducted primarily in the pursuit of educational issues and concerns. Most research is more accurately described as research *on* education, for much of it takes as its primary concern the further development of a social science discipline or, occasionally the pursuit of social policy. Over the years 'education' has thus come to be seen as a field of applied research, lacking its own distinctive theoretical structure and coherence and essentially dependent on the social sciences for its ideas and its methods.

Dilemmas in course design and course planning

Those organizing, planning and teaching courses which include a research task to be carried out by the students face a number of critical dilemmas. These dilemmas result in part from what might be conceived as fundamental differences between the nature of research and the nature of teaching as intellectual and social processes.

The research process is essentially disruptive of common sense and of the *status quo*. Much research activity is given to analysis: to taking apart taken-for-granted understanding, to the replacement of certain knowledge by a sense of indeterminacy. On the contrary, as commonly practised, much teaching is concerned with integration, with the selection and condensation of received knowledge, even at the cost of over-simplification. Conceived in these terms 'research' is essentially an experimental activity, and 'teaching' concerned primarily with theory. This is a contentious view but it reveals the nature of a dialectic which is implicit in the nature of research-based teaching.

Specifically, the dilemmas that arise are as follows:

1. 'Experience v. instruction'. In planning courses you face a decision about how to sequence first-hand experience of research and instruction in research methods and techniques. Put at its simplest, *do you (a) begin by immersing students in research projects, providing instruction in research methods only when this is requested or seems necessary, or (b) begin by providing instruction in research methods followed by gradual practice in actual cases?*

Immersion in real research has the advantage of providing strong criteria of relevance – if the research problem is given primacy, it is less likely that inappropriate instruction will be provided. Incidentally, it is an approach which vests a good deal of authority in the students as opposed to the tutor. The students will be the people who have first-hand experience of the problem and its context, and the onus will be on them to communicate issues, difficulties and concerns to their tutors. This places the tutor in a responsive rather than an instructional role, a pressure that will be increased by the somewhat eclectic way in which problems naturally present themselves. It almost certainly requires the tutor to draw on recent experience in a range of similar research situations, for the kind of information needed to contain the teaching situation is not of a kind readily available in books. This is particularly the case when the research is initiated and conceived by students rather than tutors.

This immersion approach is one that may generate considerable uncertainty and anxiety on the part of the students, but it does have the advantage of taking students closer to the experience of doing research, and so to problems of process. It is also an approach which may generate considerable motivation and commitment in those who manage it most ably and confidently.

The main advantage of the other approach is that, by beginning with a period of instruction, students become aware of the possibilities and limitations of research before facing problems in the field. Thus in the use of testing and survey methods, and in experimental studies, the period of instruction in which students typically engage before starting their own studies serves to restrict their efforts to manageable, relatively unambitious tasks which might realistically be achieved within the time and resources available. In relation to some well-developed areas this may be in fact to restrict 'hands-on' experience to doctoral students, but in doing so to ensure a degree of quality control. While this is an approach which is inevitably restricting and convergent, it does offer clarity of purpose, a linear curriculum and clear assessment procedures. The greatest danger comes from the tendency to transform educational problems into academic or technical problems.

The two approaches to research I have outlined are not in fact as incompatible as I have made them seem. However, it could be claimed that 'immersion' is generally better suited to the teaching and use of qualitative methods, which are typically inextricably related to their context of use and difficult to teach in a vacuum. Similarly, 'instruction' may be better suited to the use of quantitative approaches, which tend to lose their power when left to the vagaries of a discovery approach. I would not want to make too much of this point, however, since some exceptional researchers are, in practice, able to reverse this general conclusion. In deciding on an appropriate approach other factors also need to be considered. Full-time and part-time students may require different approaches. Doing research in one's own classroom or school is different from researching in someone else's. And from the tutor's point of view it is important to take account of the prior expectations, motivations, skills and understanding of the students.

2.   A second major dilemma concerns the choice of an appropriate pedagogy: *to what extent should you set individual assignments as opposed to group projects which will require students to work co-operatively?*

Carrying out group projects may be more complex and difficult than it might first sound. In social terms individual and group tasks are of a quite different character. My own experience of trying to establish groups which share experience and learn co-operatively is that they may generate considerable competitiveness, especially when the criteria of success are ambiguous or unclear. Nevertheless, strong group coherence offers support for students working in circumstances which increase their sense of vulnerability or uncertainty. It provides a valuable check on impetuous action and it may make the group project a happy and productive experience, even when the research itself does not work out too well. Individualization, on the other hand, can lead to isolation, it requires certain reserves of motivation, commitment and self-awareness, but does offer a degree of autonomy and a creative freedom not easily found within a close working group. The main difficulty with individual assignments is creating conditions that allow students to learn from each other's experience.

To complicate the issue there are two further aspects to the dilemma. One is the degree to which the tasks are individually allocated or chosen, the other the extent to which the task as a whole is discussed and shared by the group. It is possible to set students individual tasks, but to require them to discuss their progress within a group, just as it is possible to set group tasks but to reduce the formal time available for sharing the experience.

3.   *Should research projects be set or encouraged which focus on the particularities of specific situations? Or should projects been seen in relation to generalized, propositional knowledge? In short, should the concern be with cases or with samples?*

When the research task concentrates on issues or concerns that arise directly from practice in the classroom or the school there is frequently strong pressure to develop it as case–study research. This can lead to a tension between the demands of courses (especially the assessment demands), the experience and interests of tutors, and more general expectations as to what is appropriate within academic or professional training.

On the other hand, to give too much play to the demands of testing programmes, survey research or clinical approaches may be to commit methodological violence on substantive issues and concerns.

4.   *Which should have priority: short-term needs or long-term values?*

Conventionally, we tend to plan courses primarily in terms of what it is that we know that we think we ought to teach to students. Operating from the security of such a knowledge base we slice off segments and break off fragments that we think are appropriately taught to particular groups of students, and we organize these bits of knowledge into as coherent a programme as is possible. Research–based courses provide the starting point for another way of looking at the job of course construction and course planning. In such courses we can begin to think of designing courses which start from presenting problems, issues and topics provided by students.

The problem with courses of this kind is that the essential curriculum of courses of the first kind may become the hidden curriculum in courses of the second kind. That is to say, the propositional knowledge that is in the head of the tutor tends to be suppressed, or to become implicit, when actual problems come to dominate the curriculum. Tutors in such circumstances tend to feel that they need to hold back the knowledge which conventionally would be centrally displayed, and this can lead to puzzlement and confusion in the minds of students. 'Why did you let us go on talking when you knew what we were saying was really rubbish? We came on the course to hear your point of view, not each others', and to hide it from us is patronising. It is as if you were saying you don't think we are able to reject what you have to say and need protecting from it.' This was the comment one student made on a course I taught.

5.   *Should our first concern be to provide a professional service, or should it be to provide qualifications and awards?*

The issue here is one which reveals competing views of professionalism. One view has altruism as its central value, and sees teachers' engagement in in-service education as a necessary part of the teaching role. The other view is essentially bureaucratic, and some would say realistic. It starts from the assumption that teachers attend courses primarily in order to gain qualifications which will enhance their career prospects. In any group of students these motives will doubtless be present in varying degrees, and most people will feel both apply to some degree to their own reasons for wanting to do a particular course. More to the point here is which motive is perceived by the tutor to dominate a particular group of students, and which motives s/he can draw most strongly on in designing and teaching the course. According to the view the tutor takes, so the organization and teaching of the course will be affected.

6.   *What is the central educational purpose of the course?*

This dilemma picks up some of the issues mentioned earlier. It is possible to design a course with the central educational purpose of providing teachers with points from which to start developing and incorporating a research dimension within their professional role. This is rather different to the view that research offers teachers access to scientific knowledge which in turn offers a more rational basis for action. In terms of how to teach, what to teach and how to assess it, the first option places priority on the development of attitudes, skills and motivation (on research potential). The second points to academic competence and 'soundness'. According to the stance taken by the tutor the course is likely to evolve in very different ways, and be perceived very differently by its students. Needless to say, assessment issues follow closely on this dilemma – how do you begin to assess 'research potential'?

7.   *How do you identify appropriate audiences?*

In carrying out research projects and research assignments the issue of audience is usually a crucial one. Teachers may carry out research for themselves, for those who work with them in their own schools, for someone else conceived abstractly, or someone else conceived specifically (the chief adviser, the course tutor or the external examiner). How this dilemma is resolved has considerable consequences for the range and scope of the task, and for what are considered appropriate tasks, formats, styles of presentation and procedural considerations.

To take an example, the dissertation which often forms the central research project in research-based courses is usually primarily conceived of as an exercise for the writer-as-audience. Given the expectations that this format creates, the kind of short, unelaborated and unqualified documents which might provide the most appropriate input to a school staff meeting tend to be under-rated in the assessment process. Conventionally, we require students to elaborate beyond the call of everyday communications in the dissertation; to justify actions taken, not just to describe them; to qualify where normally it might seem reasonable to extrapolate or at least take for granted. In academic terms these things become in themselves part of the taken-for-granted expectations of the dissertation and thesis. But when we set students research tasks which set out to identify and communicate with other audiences, especially those of a policy-orientated kind, these same values may become inappropriate. School or LEA committees may well admire the sharp, brief summary from which the ambiguity and confusion and detail have been excised. As assessors we may then find ourselves with the problem of applying assessment criteria that are unfamiliar. How do you assess students for their wisdom in deciding to leave things out?

For their tact? For their ability to provide a balanced account rather than an accurate or truthful account?

The dilemmas outlined here are not exhaustive, nor are their implications fully developed. My purpose in setting them down is to give some indication of the pervasive nature of the shift to a research-based course. The different ways in which these dilemmas are resolved can lead to wide variety of aspiration and usage: a parallel example exists in the use made of 'practicals' in science teaching. There are many ways that research might be used in the context of taught courses, and most of them remain undeveloped, unexplored and untested.

2 Tasks and procedures

In this chapter I want to turn to the problem of how to find and identify appropriate tasks for research. Discussion of the origins and sources of research problems leads to a consideration of the kinds of difficulties that arise when teachers become involved in research tasks that may be interventive both in their own practice and in the functioning of the schools in which they work. Procedures that are familiar in conventional research take on new connotations when the context is one of applied research and action, so that while the labels may be familiar – confidentiality, anonymity, negotiation and clearance – they may need to be reassessed in the light of the particular difficulties that arise in such circumstances.

The origins of research tasks

It is useful at this point to identify four possible sources of research tasks: the research literature, methodological issues, problems of practice and commissions.

The research literature provides a starting point for much research. Typically the task emerges from a careful reading of the available studies in a particular field or sub-field or in reading around a particular topic, theme or problem. And usually it emerges from a gap or gaps that are perceived in the available literature. These gaps may be of a substantive kind (that there are many studies of boys' peer group culture but few of girls'), they may be gaps in the design of existing studies (there are many survey studies of heads and principals but very few observational studies), or they may result from theory running ahead of practice (for instance speculative developments in cognitive psychology which lack empirical testing).

While the research literature provides a conventional starting point for empirical work, it is one that places considerable demands and discipline on the researcher. First it requires thorough understanding of the area of the literature concerned, second it requires considerable background knowledge of the relevant discipline, third it requires technical proficiency and fourth it requires time and resources.

Perhaps not surprisingly it is relatively rare for original research of this kind to be carried out below the level of PhD; indeed many examiners discourage. students from going beyond the stage of reviewing the literature in advanced taught courses, taking the view that any empirical research that is carried out should be done in the spirit of practice exercises.

While this is an understandable position to take from a stance within the academic discipline, it is not one that accords well with the need to respond to the press of practical school research problems such as I outlined in Chapter 1. It follows that generally in applied research and action research, the research literature provides a background resource rather than the essential starting point for research designs.

One response to this problem is to design courses which, rather than starting from a base in the discipline, begin with method and technique. Colin Hook (1981) and Boehm and Weinberg (1977) both provide examples of texts that might be used as the basis for courses in classroom observation. Both books start from the practical difficulties that arise in using various observational instruments, and provide the student with a sense of what can and cannot be done with different approaches, methods and techniques. In both cases the underlying theory is derived essentially from social psychology, but this is not made explicit and forms something of a 'hidden curriculum'. The surface curriculum is one that concerns itself with learning to use research skills and treats these as though they could be disconnected from their parent discipline.

Sometimes this approach is criticized for adopting a view of research in which methods and techniques dominate, leading the researcher to frame problems to fit available methods rather than vice versa. This is always a problem in research, and in many ways much less of a problem in low-technology research such as typically is carried out in education and the social sciences than it is in science.

The third source of research tasks I identified is that of research emerging from problems of practice. Not all problems emerging from practice lend themselves to a research approach, but many do. Often such research is framed in relation to a decision. For example, if the school is considering offering a new language course, for instance in Russian, it might survey pupils and parents to gauge the likely support for the course. Having introduced the course it might turn to research in order to assess its success and locate its failings.

There may well be interaction between the three approaches I have mentioned, so that what begins as a problem that has emerged from practice might be related to a relevant area of the literature and to a set of appropriate techniques. Indeed many tutors see their function as one of helping to build these connections and to direct students in such a way that they move between these different sources. There is, though, a danger that in this process the research literature tends to dominate, or at least to become a maze which once entered is difficult to retreat from. Finding a balance that tips more towards problems and issues of an applied kind is difficult, not least because of the grip that the assessment process has on the curriculum. That is to say, because it is usually the tutor who assesses the work the academic perspective takes on additional significance and authority.

A further difficulty that frequently emerges in attempting to carry out applied research comes from trying to find a fit between the logic implicit in a presenting problem, and the assessment as to what is feasible within finite and limited resources. The scaling down of the problem to fit the requirements of the possible can lead to its translation into a different problem. This is not an uncommon difficulty, as the lack of fit between the aspirations implicit in many book titles and the reality of their contents reveals!

One way of responding to this somewhat intractable problem is to involve those who are the subjects of the research in roles where they can have more direct access to the research process, and especially to that part of the process which is concerned with the definition of the task and the design and conduct of the research. Practically one way this can be done is by relating research to a process of commissioning, which has the added advantage of shifting authority away from the tutor and more towards those devising the commission.

This use of commissions is not a familiar one in the context of teaching and so an example might clarify how it might work. The following letter was sent out to a number of educational institutions in the Norwich area and a follow-up letter sent sometime later:

Dear ——

Full-time MA Course 8 February 1982–19 March 1983

The MA (Applied Research in Education) is a one year, full-time course for experienced teachers on secondment. During the Spring Term we ask the students to work in groups of two, three or four on a commission given to them by a local school. We want the students to gain experience of working (under close supervision) on a real task. We expect them to collect information primarily by observation and by interview (though in some cases they may also use such techniques as photography or video-recording). We also place a heavy emphasis on writing, presenting and discussing a report with those who are involved in the commission.

Students are assessed on this part of the MA course, but the main criteria used in assessment are the extent to which their work meets the needs of the commission, and their ability to act professionally in a challenging role.

What we offer is a free service (albeit on a shoestring budget), access to the time and skills of other teachers who will take an interest in your work and yet take great care over any issues of confidentiality or institutional sensitivity that might arise, and at the end of the exercise a report which you may use as you wish. While we need to retain a copy of the report for assessment purposes, we undertake not to use it for any other purpose, and hope that you will treat it as belonging to you rather than to us.

We are interested in receiving either open invitations, a range of options or highly specified proposals. In the past students have

– looked at the organization of reading in an open plan First School.

- evaluated courses at the Teachers' Centre, a course for managers in local industry, and the work of the theatre-in-education group.
- collected evidence of fifth-year leavers' attitudes to school for an internal secondary school committee.
- looked at problems of communication within a Middle School.
- helped a First School reconsider its policies on remedial provision.
- helped a Remand Centre with its curriculum for short-stay inmates.

We are interested in receiving a wide range of commissions, inside and outside normal educational settings. We cannot promise to take you up on any task you set us, as the choice of commission is ultimately the responsibility of the students, but we will do what we can to help. If you have a commission, or would like to talk the idea over, please contact me as soon as possible.

Rob Walker
Course Tutor
November 1981

Dear ——

I would like to thank all those who were involved in providing us with commissions and tasks for the full-time MA group this year. In the event we received the following requests:

- from a Primary School to examine their Environmental Studies curriculum.
- from a Junior School to investigate the possibility of establishing a resource room in the school.
- an open commission from a High School to be negotiated with a group of Heads of Department.
- a similar response from another High School.
- a commission from the Adult Education Department to interview all those Adult Education tutors who had attended a phase 1 Training Course last year.
- we were asked to look at a special course for unemployed young offenders.
- a Football Club provided the opportunity to study their youth liaison programme.

— An FE College asked us to evaluate courses for disadvantaged school leavers.

— a Social Services Department asked us to look at educational provision in Adult Training Centres.

I was most encouraged by the range and interest inherent in these possibilities, and only sorry that we could not take on all of them. Needless to say, it presented us with difficult decisions, and I have taken the unusual step this year of sending you a copy of the list so that you can see just how wide-ranging the responses to my earlier letter were. To those whose offers we are unable to take up we hope we may respond in the future if suitable opportunities arise. In the meantime I would like to thank you for your help, and for making the MA course's decision so difficult to make!

Yours sincerely
Rob Walker
Course Tutor

Approaches like the above are most appropriate when the students are on full-time secondment and are able to devote blocks of (day)time to working in other institutions. Working outside one's own institution becomes more difficult for teachers studying part-time, more often than not with no day release. The general principle, however, may still hold. Rather than circulating a range of institutions with the request for commissions it might be possible to circulate a number of groups and individuals within the school, or less formally simply to ask people what might be of use to them. The point is to create research situations where the task is negotiated with someone, or a group, who provides the initial commission, a starting point that sets in train a series of negotiations that mark this kind of task out from the other kinds I have mentioned.

The aim here is to create situations which provide students with minimum starting points. There is no hidden 'right answer', no readily available literature at hand, no obvious techniques to be applied. Instead the student has to work to organize the task and decide on procedure given limited time and limited resources. I believe this is important because when I have tried to teach research from existing resources I have often found it difficult to establish that research always takes place in a bounded context where these kinds of constraints are more important at the time than they might seem in retrospect. As a result I have found students frequently planning unrealistic projects and dissertations, simply because they have little idea what is possible within finite resources. The idea of starting from a commission is in part to place people in situations where they have to make decisions about priorities in the face of conflicting expectations (at the very least there is a conflict between what the commissioners ask for and what an ideal research model can provide). The effect is to open up a world that is often hidden to all those who use research but do not practise it, for in fact all research projects are faced with such decisions, though they do not always report them or report them in a way that reveals them to the inexperienced reader.

Beginning from a letter like the one illustrated above establishes an initial situation within which schools and researchers need to communicate in order to arrive at a task which is both feasible and useful. It assumes too that this communication must be two-way and not simply one where the researcher has a design to 'sell' and the school chooses whether or not to allow access. When a commission is involved the school inevitably gets drawn into taking some responsibility for the purpose and content of the research, and the researcher is drawn into considering the school as an audience as well as a subject.

In this sense, using the commission as a starting point for research is to narrow the distinction between a research project and an evaluation. Commissioned research and evaluation remain however as distinct, for commissioned research allows for much greater flexibility on both sides in terms of shifting the focus of the study or changing its concerns. Nevertheless, in approaching a commissioning agency (whether it be a school or other group) it may be useful to bear in mind some of the questions that evaluators typically take with them into the field.

The following list was devised by Joseph Millman. It was originally intended as a checklist for assessing evaluation reports, but is perhaps even more helpful for use in prospect rather than in retrospect. ('p/p' refers to 'programme/product' and is intended as shorthand for the subject of the evaluation exercise. To translate the checklist into the present context, p/p has to be variously translated as the research commission, problem, task, question, design or report.)

The checklist

I. *Preconditions of the p/p*

How well did the evaluator assess (or provide information on):
A. Need for the p/p
1. What was needed (need for the program per se/need for anticipated program effects)?
2. Who needed the p/p?
3. How much (scope/depth) was needed and when?
4. Why was the p/p needed (moral, programmatic, empirical, legal, political, social, or philosophical justifications)?
5. What is the value of the p/p even if it could do all that is hoped for it (content analysis of the worth of the p/p and importance of the needs interfaced with items IA 1–4 above)?
B. Market for the p/p
1. Who will use the p/p?
2. How many will use the p/p?
C. Dissemination plan of the p/p
1. How will the p/p reach the market?
2. Are any implementation and delivery problems expected?

II. *Effects of the p/p*

How well did the evaluator assess (or provide information on):
A. Indicators used in the evaluation
1. What are the indicators of the intended p/p outcomes?
2. What are the characteristics of these indicators (comprehensiveness, ability to diagnose strengths and weaknesses, validity, reliability, credibility)?
3. Were side effects of the p/p searched for?
4. Was the operation or process of the p/p observed (adherence to legal, ethical, and moral standards: congruence with stated claims for the p/p; documentation the treatment actually took place)?
B. Causative claims (internal validity)
1. Do testing, selection, regression, and other factors jeopardize the validity of causal claims of effectiveness of the p/p?

2. What was the sampling error (statistical significance/-results due to chance)?

C. Generalization of results (external validity)
   1. Were field tests under conditions in which the p/p is to be used (typical users, time frame, settings, and the like/special circumstances and talent used: Hawthorne effect)?
   2. Are the effects of the p/p likely to last?

D. Analysis of the data
   1. Were p/p performance data appropriately treated (that is, transformed, analyzed)?
   2. What was the magnitude of the effects of the p/p?
   3. Was there attention to both hard and soft data with respect to the p/p?

III. Utility of the p/p

How well did the evaluator assess (or provide information on):

A. Cost of the p/p
   1. What were the 'direct' costs of the p/p (fixed/variable; initial running; depreciation/amortization)?
   2. What were the opportunity costs of the p/p (time, forgone benefits)?
   3. Who really pays for the p/p (funding agency, developer, taxpayer, user, and so on)?

B. Benefit of the p/p
   1. Were performance and cost data of the p/p synthesized?
   2. What was the social or educational significance of the effects of the p/p?
   3. Was the value of the p/p compared to the value of real and possible alternative p/ps, recognized or not (crucial competitors)?
   4. What is the future or potential utility of the p/p (likelihood of extended support, availability, maintenance, updates, and so on)?

IV. Preconditions (for the evaluation)

A. Need for the evaluation
   1. Who wanted the evaluation?
   2. For what purposes?
   3. Were other relevant audiences identified?
   4. Was the evaluation likely to be used?
   5. Were the interests, perspectives, resources, options, decisions, potential payoffs and hazards, and so on identified?

B. Appropriateness of agreement and timing for the evaluation
1. Were important expectations and responsibilities agreed upon (data access, cooperation of affected parties, resources, timeline, length of report, anonymity, control of bias in data collection and reporting, provisions for amendments, final editorial authority by the evaluator, release of results, audiences for the report)?
2. Was the p/p in place long enough for a summative evaluation to be appropriate?

V. Effects (of the evaluation)

A. Intended effects of the evaluation
1. What was the nature of the intended effects (decision making, improved understandings, information, conflict resolution, complacency reduction)?
2. What were the evaluator's judgements (what did the evaluator say the implications were, conditions under which the p/p might be successful, statements about crucial competitors)?
B. Side effects of the evaluation
1. What were the positive side effects (knowledge beyond the setting in which the p/p was applied, provided a generalizable process of evaluation model, initiated a built-in mechanism for evaluation of p/p, left behind an evaluative intelligence, stimulated further inquiry, and so on)?
2. What were the negative side effects (alienation of staff and clients, left scene with 'dirty hands,' and so on)?
C. Impact reducing factors of the evaluation
1. What context factors affected the evaluation's impact (social and political milieu under which evaluator operated)?
2. How did the evaluator's conduct affect the evaluation's impact (adherence/nonadherence of evaluator to social, political, legal, contractual, and ethical standards)?
3. Did the oral presentation or written report reduce or enhance the evaluation's impact (length, clarity, style, and so on)?
4. Is there potential for evaluation impact (will evaluator or p/p staff be around to follow through on recommendations, track record of the evaluator, and the like)?

VI. Utility (of the evaluation)

   A. Cost of the evaluation
      1. Did the evaluation pay for itself?
      2. Was there flagrant overspending (every-pupil testing, waste motion, and the like)?
   B. Benefit of the evaluation
      1. Congruence of evaluator's claims to client needs?
      2. Social or educational significance of the effect of the evaluation?
      3. Comparative value to other evaluation designs that might have been employed?

(Millman, 1981, 316–18)

Millman's list makes the question of utility more complicated than it might at first seem. There is more to it than hoping that what you are doing is of some use to someone, though inevitably such acts of faith remain significant elements in most research studies.

Problems of procedure

ACCESS

In discussing the kinds of tasks that might provide starting-points for research I have already indicated that access raises different problems according to the approach adopted. If you are beginning from a starting-point in the literature the main problem of negotiating access to data is determined by a sampling design. Usually quite precise requirements can be specified in advance of the study, for example whether or not questionnaires will be used, what the purpose of the study is intended to be, what kind of information will be collected and how it will be used, and so on. All these questions are treated as technical questions and within the control of the researcher. The access problem consists in the main in persuading people to let you enter their schools and classrooms, fill in your questionnaires or administer your tests to their children. Even when the task is conceived in qualitative terms the situation is broadly the same, the intentions of the research and the appropriateness of the design are problems that lie with the researcher, and the access problem is conceived in terms of persuading people to let you in.

The same points hold when the starting point is primarily methodological, though it may be a little more difficult to persuade people to give you access to their schools and classrooms on what amounts to a blank cheque, for the intentions and outcomes of the research will not be so closely specified or so clear to those who are to be its subjects.

Beginning from problems of practice does have the considerable advantage of being able to present the project as one which emerges from a real teaching problem, and one which for the most part people will recognize. Initial access is therefore likely to be relatively easy, provided the problem is not one which people feel has heavy political implications.

Access is even likely to be an issue for those beginning from a commission, for while the commission might seem at first to present a contract which guarantees access, it is usual for commissions to involve the collection of information from others who may not have been party to the original commission. Take, for example, the first two commissions mentioned in the second letter above: one to evaluate an environmental studies curriculum, the other to look at resource centres. Both originated from the heads of the schools and had then to be negotiated with teachers, children and parents within a context of sponsorship by the headteacher. In this sense commissions may not be quite as straightforward an entrée as they might seem at first sight, and indeed it is not uncommon for much of the research to be taken up with the problem of unravelling the full implications of the relationship between the commissioner and those who are the subjects and audience for the research.

CONFIDENTIALITY AND ANONYMITY

Confidentiality and anonymity present variable difficulties according to the starting point for the research. For the literature-derived study which sees its final destination as feeding back into the literature, the problem may be relatively routine. Generally in such cases there is no problem in hiding the identity of those who are the subjects of research and in reporting in such a way that they are not identifiable. But I hesitate because non–identifiability is not so easily guaranteed as we are sometimes tempted to assume. This is especially the case when the final account is of a descriptive or case study kind in which people are likely to be identifiable to themselves and to each other even when their names have been changed and they are well disguised from strangers. This becomes a more acute problem when those who are the subjects of the study are also one of its primary audiences. In this case simply changing names is likely to have little value, except in the case of a document 'leaking' to those outside the study.

This is an area where researchers themselves disagree. Elizabeth Richardson, in her study of Nailsea School (Richardson, 1973), took an unusually strong stand on the issue:

During all these preliminary negotiations [with the school] I was aware many times of being under a subtle kind of pressure to give assurances about scientific objectivity, about protective anonymity, and about tangible results in the shape of solutions to problems, pressures which I found it by no means easy to resist. Yet I felt it was important to begin as I meant to go on. Firstly, I did not attempt to deny that my approach would inevitably contain a large element of subjectivity, since I would be coming into the situation as the person I was, with previous experiences that would affect my view of events. I had to acknowledge that the kind of interpretations I should be trying to make of unconscious as well as conscious feelings, beliefs and attitudes within the staff group, being largely intuitive, would by their very nature be incapable of the kind of 'proof' that scientists normally looked for in their work. At best, I should be seeking for evidence, through people's words, actions and interactions, that might confirm or refute my assessment of situations. Secondly, I made it clear right at the beginning that if, as I hoped, the work culminated in a published report or book, I should want the school to be named, since 'anonymity' in research projects of this kind could never in any event be total. Moreover, my view of 'anonymity', which I expressed then and still adhere to now, is that it can too easily be used as a protective device – a device that in fact endangers the school while it protects the research worker; for, in maintaining the apparent 'anonymity' of the institution he works with, the researcher may emerge as a betrayer of confidence, having avoided the painful process of working through with the teachers who have collaborated with him the material he wants to publish about them. Once it is agreed that the school is to be named, everyone who is at any time during the project involved in recorded events has a responsibility to accept or reject what is being said about the institution. And in working together at the disagreement, teacher and researcher may arrive at a more accurate and illuminating view of the situation being described. Thirdly, I tried to emphasize at this early stage that I could not give any guarantee that any solutions to emerging problems would be found; all I could hope was that I might, by working on the boundary of the school, be able to help the staff themselves to clarify the nature of those problems, the better to arrive at their own measures for tackling them.

(Richardson, 1973, 44–5)

Richardson is probably right in claiming that anonymity has often been used in the past as a means of protecting the researcher under the guise of offering protection to those who are the subjects of the study. Her argument, though, has not persuaded many to follow her practice, perhaps in part because researchers have been reluctant to engage in 'the painful process of working through with the teachers who have collaborated with him the material he wants to publish about them', but also because many have felt that identification carries with it a number of risks that are not entirely predictable. Even if subjects and the researcher agree to publish, there is no telling what the consequences might be for the subjects in terms of future career prospects, in terms of continuing to work in situations that have become exposed, or even in terms of a wider public response.

These problems become magnified in documentary films, a number of which have been made in schools, especially for television audiences. Roger Graef's film in his *Space Between Words* series made for BBC television brought public pressure to bear on the teacher who was featured in it. More recently Richard Denton's films *Public School* and *Kingswood*, also made for the BBC, have attracted considerable attention. Apparently the BBC went to some lengths in these cases to prepare people for the likely public reaction, but Brian Tyler, head of Kingswood, has said that despite the preparation, the few abusive letters he received amongst a mail that was mostly positive or constructively critical, did hurt and disturb him. This might seem a risk that is worth taking in the context of film-making. In research, however, we have a choice. We can disguise and hide identities in anonymity, and faced with uncertainty about possible repercussions of disclosure most of us, most of the time, choose to use some degree of protection. Elizabeth Richardson's argument is unusual but it is a powerful one and not easy for people to resist. Potential subjects wanting to take issue with it may seem to have something to hide and so are necessarily put at something of a disadvantage in negotiating a contract with a researcher. This, added to the pressure that a staff peer group can generate, often means that individuals may find it hard to argue against a position agreed, say, between the head and the researcher.

The main danger for most studies is not that of mass exposure so much as local and immediate circulation or availability. In its way this may be even more interventive, for if studies made in schools and classrooms of a local authority become easily available to teachers and other employees then this may disturb existing patterns of relationships. This is especially the case in the context of a course whose members include not only teachers and heads but prominent union members and local advisers. Indeed, one tutor has in the past suspected that the local authority encouraged a teacher to apply for a particular course because 'they wanted to find out more about the school'. This problem extends beyond research-based courses, for this kind of disclosure can always emerge in discussion. Courses like those described in this book are, however, particularly vulnerable because such information is moved from the area of gossip and social talk onto the agenda, making it more difficult for people to present calculated images or to avoid critical questioning.

Overall the most important point to make is that anonymity and confidentiality are not easily handled by established procedures or by standardized codes of practice. They are rather active issues that need to be carefully considered case by case. It is also important to build this point into the curriculum of the course, so that students come to share a concern for the issues.

NEGOTIATION AND REPORTING

'Negotiation' is important at most stages of the research process. The initial task usually emerges from some kind of negotiation process conducted with a tutor and/or with a school or a group of teachers. Even when the task is one which imposes a rigid design and closely specifies a sample and methods of data collection, some negotiation will inevitably be necessary in order to operationalize the design in actual circumstances. Finding time and people and appropriate circumstances is rarely easy in the complex routines of the secondary school day, and it can be difficult too in the rather different circumstances of primary schools.

Here I am assuming that negotiation will continue beyond the stage of obtaining access and putting the design into operation, and that in many cases the negotiation process will lead to changes in research that are of a substantive kind. Educational research is unusual because it is an integral part of the process it seeks to study, and there are more or less direct interconnections between research and practice. In this sense it is unlike many areas of the social sciences, which have in effect cut themselves off from worlds of practice by a series of boundaries. It is not possible for an educational researcher to study what goes on in schools and classrooms with the same naivety or objectivity which characterizes research in other fields. It is particularly difficult for teachers studying for further qualifications to do so because they have less excuse for being ill-informed or lacking in understanding in the ways and worlds of schooling. Educational research almost always takes place therefore against what Lawrence Stenhouse has called (borrowing the term from history) a 'second record' (Stenhouse, 1978): a second record that is particularly powerful and prominent for teachers-as-researchers because it provides the main medium of continuity and communication with those who become the subjects of their research.

This raises again the point noted earlier, namely that there is a particular problem for research which consists in the main of teachers looking at teaching: that the interests and concerns of others, and particularly of pupils and parents, can become squeezed out, or else reinterpreted in terms of a teacher perspective. That is to say, it is particularly difficult for teachers to talk to and negotiate with pupils and parents in a research role without letting their teacher role intrude. It is possible to adopt procedures which minimize the difficulty, but it remains one that persists and recurs; at the very least it involves the researcher-teacher in incipient schizophrenia (perhaps 'conflict of roles' is a more accurate and less emotive way of putting it): a state which is likely to cause confusion amongst those who are the subjects of the research and who are unlikely to be able to draw quite so fine distinctions as the researcher.

I say this on the assumption that what is changed most by research is the researcher – it is almost always the researcher who learns most, changes most, has most commitment to the project and most at stake if it fails. Even when the intention (as in many evaluation studies) is to act in a service role and to remain independent and objective, this remains true. In fact the main need for 'objectivity' may be to protect the researcher rather than the researched. Most subjects (despite what I have said about the need to establish a safety net of procedures) are well able to look after their own interests. It is the researcher who is vulnerable, and often does not see it. It is the researcher who is isolated and obsessive, working in places where in one sense he or she has little right to be, and so is constantly pitched into precarious and thinly held relations with others. As Elizabeth Richardson suggests, it is the researcher who tends to run for cover.

On the other hand many researchers and evaluators have argued for extensive controls on the research process in order to curb its interventive effects. Stephen Kemmis and Ian Robottom, for example, have outlined the following contract for evaluators negotiating with their subjects:

Principles of procedure

(a) Independence

(i) No participant in the project will have privileged access to the data of the evaluation.
(ii) No participant will have a unilateral right or power of veto over the content of the report.

(b) Disinterest

(i) The evaluator will attempt to represent, as widely as possible, the range of viewpoints encountered in the evaluation, rather than to enunciate his own perspectives or private views.

(ii) The evaluator recognizes that explicit or implicit recommendations appearing in reports will not be regarded as prescriptions
by programme participants. As far as possible, however, the
evaluator will attempt to present recommendations from
participants rather than to use the evaluation as a platform for his
own preferences.

(c) Negotiated access

The evaluation will seek only 'reasonable access' to relevant data
sources. The evaluator will assume he can freely approach any
individual involved in the project to collect data. Those
approached should feel free to discuss any matters they see fit. All
such discussions will be treated as privileged by the evaluator. The
evaluator is bound to portray the project and the issues it raises,
but the release of specific information likely to identify informants
will be subject to negotiation with these informants.

(d) Negotiation of boundaries

(i) The evaluation will be issues-oriented. The principles for
inclusion of concerns, perspectives or information in the study or
its reports are that these concerns, perspectives or items of
information contribute to understanding the project, especially in
so far as it is variously understood by participants in and observers
of the project from their different points of view. A major task for
the evaluation, therefore, is to attempt to piece these disparate
perspectives together into a coherent (though not necessarily
synthetic or 'complete') account of the project as a whole. Thus
according to this principle of inclusion, the perspectives of all
participants and interested observers have a 'right to be con
sidered' in the evaluation.

(ii) The principle for exclusion of concerns, perspectives or
information is that they can be shown to be false or unfounded,
irrelevant to the project, or to unfairly disadvantage individuals or
groups involved with the project.

(e) Negotiation of accounts

(i) The criteria of fairness, relevance and accuracy form the basis for
negotiation between the evaluator and participants in the study.
Where accounts of the work of participants' involvement in the
project can be shown to be unfair, irrelevant or inaccurate, the
report will be amended. Once draft reports have been negotiated
with participants on the basis of these criteria, they will be
regarded as having the endorsement of those involved in the
negotiations with respect to fairness, relevance and accuracy.

(ii) The process of negotiation of accounts will, where necessary, be phased to protect participants from the consequences of one-way information flow. Parts of a report may first be negotiated with relevant individuals who could be disadvantaged if the report were negotiated as a whole with all participants.

(f) Negotiation of release

(i) There will be no secret reporting. Reports will be made available first to those whose work they represent. Circulation will be phased so that members of the primary audience will receive reports earliest, with other audiences receiving them later.

(ii) The release of reports for circulation beyond the community of interests formed by members of the primary audience and the evaluator is a matter for negotiation and decision within this community of interests. Given that the reports have been 'endorsed' as fair, relevant and accurate by the procedure of negotiation of accounts, release of reports may be delayed or restricted only if it can be shown that release of a report to secondary or other audiences would unfairly disadvantage any member of the primary audience. In this case, an amended version of the report may be prepared which would overcome this obstacle to its release, viz. a version of the report which does not, by its release, disadvantage any member of the primary audience. Any such amended version must still be acceptable to the primary audience as a fair, relevant and accurate account of the project, however.

(iii) In keeping with the foregoing principles of procedure, the circulation of reports will be restricted unless the report has been cleared for unrestricted circulaton. Restriction on circulation will be clearly indicated on the cover pages of all reports..

(g) Publication

(i) Reports will be released for wider circulation only in the form established by the procedure of negotiation of accounts; that is, they must be 'endorsed' by the members of the primary and other audiences as fair, relevant and accurate. Any published report must first of all meet this criterion.

(ii) The evaluator reserves the right to disavow any incomplete or summary version of the report which purports to be a report of this evaluation.

(iii) Any report to be published should have been produced according to these principles of procedure.

(iv) It is the expectation of the evaluator that the sponsor of the evaluation will have right of first refusal on publication.

(h) Confidentiality

 (i) The evaluator will not examine files, correspondence or other documentation without explicit authorization and will not copy from those sources without permission.

 (ii) Interviews, meetings, and written exchanges will not be considered 'off-the-record', but those involved are free, both before and after, to restrict aspects or parts of such exchanges, or to correct or improve their statement. Quotations, verbatim transcripts and attributed observations, judgements, conclusions or recommendations, where these are used in such a way as to identify their sources, will be used in reports only with the authorization of the informant (i.e. the authorization achieved by the procedure of negotiation of accounts). Where information is general or where the sources are sufficiently obscured so as to defy identification of specific individuals, no clearance will be sought.

(iii) The evaluator is responsible for the confidentiality of data collected by him in the course of the evaluation.

(iv) In general, it should be noted that these confidentiality rules cannot be used to withdraw reports from general view; once fair, relevant and accurate accounts have been released and when they are presented in ways which do not unnecessarily expose or embarass participants, such reports should no longer be sheltered by the prohibitions of confidentiality.

(i) Accountability

The evaluator cannot make all his records publicly available without breaching the evaluation's principles of procedure. Nevertheless, the evaluation and the evaluator must be accountable to sponsors, project participants and the evaluation audiences. Thus:

 (i) The evaluation will keep appropriate financial and administrative records which will be open to its immediate sponsor.

 (ii) The evaluation will be accountable to participants as outlined in these principles of procedure.

(iii) The evaluator will work with an advisory committee of 'critical friends' to whom the entire evaluation process and its records, files and reports will be open in principle. The primary role of this committee is to evaluate the evaluation process, check emerging interpretations against available evidence, suggest further data-gathering activities, and to assist with the interpretation and implementation of the principles of procedure. This advisory committee will itself be bound by these principles of procedure unless they are breached by the evaluator, in which case the advisory committee will intervene to attempt to resolve problems arising by negotiation with the evaluator and relevant others.

(*j*) *Agreement to these principles of procedures*

(i) The evaluator cannot be held responsible for breaches of these principles by others involved in the evaluation. It is the responsibility of members of the primary and other audiences of the evaluation to respect the confidentiality of reports and any restrictions on their circulation.

(ii) In commissioning this evaluation study and in accepting the commission, the sponsor and the evaluator agree to abide by these principles of procedure.

(Kemmis and Robottom, 1981, 151–5)

Given this detailed specification, and comparing it with the simple blanket notion of 'trust' required by other researchers/ evaluators, you might ask why there is an apparent conflict of view over issues of objectivity, negotiation and the control of research. In part it is no doubt explained by differing intentions on the part of researchers, but also I suggest it relates to the very different tasks taken on by researchers, and more particularly to the ways in which they perceive and construct these tasks. When what is valued most is what I have loosely described as 'making a contribution to the literature', then the rights of subjects can legitimately be minimized and generalized. The research is not primarily for them, the intention is to intervene as little as possible and the main effort goes into understanding general problems. However, when the task is local and immediate and is conceived in part as a service to those who are its subjects, or to those who have immediate control over those who are the subjects, then tighter controls become necessary. In evaluation studies particularly, it is this sense of immediacy and relevance that has brought the issue to the fore, and explains the kind of detailed control that Kemmis and Robottom suggest is necessary in place of mutual trust.

There are, in the sense I have just described it, two distinct traditions in educational research, one academic and one applied. A danger I see in the increasing development of research-based courses is that most of us who teach such courses have been trained in the academic tradition, whereas most of those who are taking such courses approach them from the applied end. This can lead to some confusion over the need for the kind of procedures that have been introduced in this chapter. Some may feel that an elaborate contract of the kind that Kemmis and Robottom propose is in itself an inappropriate intervention. To raise these issues early in a project would be to alienate those who would prefer to work on a basis of trust. (On one occasion when we introduced them to a group of heads whose project we were to evaluate we were accused of using 'the language of building society surveys'.) Indeed to formalize relationships in this way might seem over-bureaucratic and lead to strain, particularly when the researcher is someone who works in the organization and is already known as a colleague and as a teacher.

On the other hand such formal statements do clarify rights and obligations and set the study on a 'professional' footing. In retrospect many people who have later run into difficulties have been glad to have such a contract to fall back on as a way of seeing them through. Whether or not to formalize relationships in contractual terms is in the end a question of judgement. Perhaps I should say *in the beginning* it is a question of judgement, for it is a judgement call that has to be made prior to action, when problems and difficulties in relationships in the negotiation of tasks and likely outcomes can only be guessed at on the basis of rapid assessments and prior experience. Each case has to be considered in its own terms.

Those of us who have worked in evaluation have tended to work from the outside on a limited term basis; we have rarely tried to do evaluation or applied research within the institutions where we work or where we teach. Yet this is precisely the situation faced by many teachers attracted by research-based courses, who often come to such courses without prior training in research, and have, as it were, to fall back on moral positions and procedural principles culled from their own experience as teachers and as members of educational organizations. This can be extremely demanding on even the best teachers, and 'failure' and mistakes, while they can provide fertile ground for learning, can become uncomfortable for the student and embarrassing for the institution.

While prudence is a virtue in this kind of research and suggests to students that it is wise to play safe, there may be other reasons why students are prepared to take risks. They may perceive, for instance, that their tutors, or the wider literature, place high value on risk-taking, individualism and creativity. To put it bluntly, no one gets an A for a routine piece of work. As a result some people get caught in a knot in which avoiding trouble is considered a necessity while taking risks is highly regarded.

I have included reporting research in this section in part because it is at the point of reporting that relationships between the researcher and the institution within which the research has been carried out most often run into difficulties. Very often these difficulties stem from the conflicting demands placed on students both to play safe and yet to take risks. Again perhaps this stems from the split I have described betweeen academic and applied research, for what we often reward in academic work is originality and imagination: challenging interpretations in the face of what at first sight appears to be relatively routine material. When these values are carried across into applied research (as I believe they often are, even to a magnified degree), then this places the student (and perhaps the professional researcher) in the position of having to play off risks taken with their relationships with those who are their subjects against risks with the presentation of their research. This may well be enhanced by the imposition of short timelines and deadlines which loom more quickly than the natural time-scale of the research suggests.

I have depicted the problems in this way because I want to emphasize again that there are few right answers or easily applied procedures. In this sense Kemmis and Robottom's list is itself misleading. Almost all the issues have to be worked through more or less continuously in any particular piece of research, and while prior contracts sometimes act as a useful safety net, they are often forgotten, misunderstood or deliberately ignored by both subjects and researchers. What is called for is active and continuous awareness of the issues coupled with as many ways of ensuring prudent action on the part of the researcher as is possible. For the tutor this raises the important problem of how to assess students for their wisdom in *not* doing things, *not* including certain material and statements in their reports and avoiding certain kinds of interpretation, rather than simply rewarding them for what they *do* include.

In this sense the checklist may not be so helpful as a case-study approach to the actual problems faced by a project or an individual in establishing a piece of research. Clem Adelman provides such an account of a project which looked at the use made of objects in nursery schools (Adelman, 1976). Here you will find a concern for many of the same issues as raised by Kemmis and Robottom, but implicit in a series of contacts with people and correspondence with authorities:

Research schedule

4 April 1974	First proposal submitted to SSRC to run from 1 September 1974 to 1 September 1976. £20,000 requested to include Research Assistant and secretary.
May 1974	First informal contacts with schools.
July 1974	First proposal not approved. SSRC suggests feasibility study of 9 months.
September 1974	Feasibility study proposal submitted. Ford Teaching Project (due to end at this time) extended to 31 December for writing up and publication.
28 October 1974	Feasibility study approved. 1 January–30 September 1975. £5,400 to include secretary two days a week. Request for access to schools submitted to County Education Officer.
January 1975	Field work in nursery school one morning and one afternoon per week and in the First school nursery one afternoon per week.

April 1975	Proposal to SSRC to extend research from 1 October 1975 to 1 October 1977. £14,500 without Research Assistant.
July 1975	Proposal not accepted. SSRC suggests an immediate proposal for up to £4,000 for 6 month extension from 1 October 1975.
18 August 1975	Permission for access to reception class approved.
Beginning September 1975	First three weeks recording in all three classrooms. Subsequently reception class and nursery school.
End September 1975	Proposal for 18 month extension from 1 April 1976 submitted to SSRC.
December 1975	Proposal approved but SSRC unable to justify priority for funding.

Strategy adopted

In May 1974, before the first Grant was approved, I made contact through an employee of Norfolk Area Health Authority with the head teacher in a nursery school, to sound out the possibility of my working with a teacher in her school. I was also interested in finding out whether the head teacher found the content of the project to be of relevance to the educational problems in the school. The head teacher was encouraging on the project's relevance, and made some useful comments. I asked her advice about which First School might be selected. She suggested the one I eventually went into. I left the head teacher with the following synopsis of the research proposal:

Educational use of objects in the nursery school

Nursery schools provide surroundings which have a wide range of plentiful objects. This proposed study is interested in how objects are used as things to be talked about, to derive tasks from, for imaginative play, etc. I am particularly interested in how teachers talk to children about the objects.

Design of the study

Initially – during the feasibility stage – one nursery class in a nursery school and one in a primary school would be involved. I would like to get to know the teachers and children before initiating any attempts at recording the activities. I would begin by observing in a participant sort of way. For instance I would respond to children's questions, requests, etc. I already have experience of using extremely unobtrusive recording techniques; the equipment is very small; no lighting or adaptations to the normal classroom are needed. These recordings would be shown back to the teachers and probably to the children for their comment and discussion.

What the study hopes to achieve:
1. A mapping of the variety, distribution and numbers of objects.
2. A comparison between the range of different sorts of use of the objects.
3. The relationship between the use of the object, the talk and socialisation of the child into the ethos of educational values.

The project will be based at the Centre for Applied Research in Education, University of East Anglia, supported by the Social Science Research Council. The feasibility study would have a duration of 6/9 months and could start any time after January 1975.

As soon as the grant had been approved, I wrote, on 28 October 1974, to the County Education Officer:

The Social Science Research Council have awarded me a grant to study the use of objects in nursery schools.

My two years at the Centre for Applied Research in Education have involved close liaison with East Anglian schools associated with the Ford Teaching Project.

I have had the pleasure to meet and talk with the heads of a First School and a nursery school. They were kind enough to provide consultation and advice about the grant proposal and are sufficiently interested in the content of the research to be prepared to offer, subject to your consent, the co-operation of their schools in what is initially a nine-month feasibility study.

I have had six years' experience of research in schools, prior to which I was a teacher for six years. Amongst my students for two of these years were nursery nurses.

Please would you give your permission for this research to commence at the end of January 1975.

Enclosed is a synopsis of the proposal. [as above]

My request for permission was passed down the line to an Assistant Education Officer. On 19 November 1974 I visited the Assistant

Education Officer. He wanted to know what the research would involve for the schools and what the end product would be. I explained the commitment the schools might have to give:

1. I would be in the schools a minimum of two half days a week in each school, and
2. in the feasibility study only one teacher from each school would be involved.

The Assistant Education Officer made the point several times that, although he thought the research was worthwhile, he did not have the power to make the final decision. He was concerned about the quality of teaching I would want to see. I offered 'teaching that was recognised as "good practice" '. (Later, visiting the First School, the headmistress told me that the Assistant Education Officer had rung to tell her that I should only see 'good practice'.) The Assistant Education Officer asked if I would work in any other First Schools if entry to that particular First School was refused. I said yes as the vital school to retain was the nursery school.

I awaited a reply from the County Education Officer. In the meantime, the Director of the Centre, Lawrence Stenhouse, sent two letters to the County Education Officer, viz:

1 December 1974

We have received a grant from the Social Science Research Council to mount a study of the use of objects in the nursery school. The grant has now been accepted by the University and the grant period begins on 1 January. I enclose the statement of this grant which we have made to the University Information Officer.

Mr Adelman, who will be doing this work, had a discussion with one of your staff, an Assistant Education Officer, about the possibility of mounting his study in a nursery school and the nursery class of a First School. The teachers in these schools, who gave Mr Adelman advice when he was drafting his proposal, are very willing that he should work with them.

I am concerned that Mr Adelman should be able to start his study after the Christmas recess, and I am writing to ask for your permission that he may go ahead in working with these schools.

Eventually, a letter dated 23 December 1974 was sent to me granting access 'under the conditions agreed during the interview on 19 November 1974'.

These conditions were:

1. To study the 'good practice' of one teacher for a maximum of two whole days a week.
2. To inform the Area Education Officer how the research was going on.

This letter awaited my return to CARE on 3 January 1975. I immediately sent letters to the two head teachers to ask them to let me know if I could visit. The head of the First School rang on 6 January to ask when I was coming in – she had not yet received my letter but had already been informed by the Assistant Education Officer that access had been granted. I arranged to visit on the 13th. I had not heard from the other head teacher and so rang her on the 14th. She apologised for not replying and said I could come at any time to suit the teacher concerned. As I was already going to visit the First School teacher on 15/16 January, the only day available was Friday 17 January.

In each of the schools I assured the head teacher and the class teacher that the information I was collecting would be confidential; that they would hold the right to refuse permission for its wider publication; that the children would only be picked out by their christian names; that the photographs would be reduced to line drawings unless specific permission was gained from the school and parents of the children involved. I explained that this was a feasibility study which might be funded further. I said that as far as possible I would provide transcripts of lessons and replay recordings to the teacher and eventually to the children and their parents. I agreed on a rough timetable for visits with the teacher. These arrangements were as far as possible adhered to, the school being contacted some days before if arrangements had to be changed.

The request to the County Education Officer to commence research in Norfolk was the first he had received from CARE since he had taken up his post during reorganisation. On 10 February Lawrence Stenhouse received a letter from the Assistant Education Officer which formalised the arrangements necessary before approval would be granted:

1. When any research project or contact with schools was envisaged or desired by members of the CARE staff, there would be an approach to the LEA in the first instance.
2. Discussion would then take place with the LEA about schools which might be suitable. This would involve the CARE staff in outlining the objectives and purpose of the research, and the situation for which they were looking and would involve the LEA in considering all other pressures on schools and any factors within the schools.
3. An agreed number of schools would be identified, and the research staff would then be able to contact the schools and discuss any proposals with the head (and teachers).
4. The LEA would then be asked to approve the final arrangements.

As part of my agreement I was to keep the Assistant Education Officer and the teachers informed about the progress of the research.

By 15 April 1975 I had to submit a further proposal to the Social Science Research Council for funds to complete the research after September 1975. I wrote on 15 May to the Assistant Education Officer thus:

> The research seems to be progressing quite well. I feel that I have a good working relationship with both teachers I am observing.
>
> They have asked me at various times what will happen after the feasibility study ends and what will be the uses of the research findings. I have had to submit a proposal for an extension of the grant to the Social Science Research Council at what is an early stage in the research. The Committee that makes the decisions on whether to support proposals meets some time in July, then again late September. The feasibility study grant terminates at the end of September.
>
> I enclose a copy of what I intend to give to the teacher and the head of each school. I hope this meets with your approval. I do realise that you mentioned that after the feasibility study the involvement of these schools would be reviewed by you. Hopefully I might be able to continue to work with these teachers one half day a week for two terms in the 1976 session. Perhaps we might arrange a meeting to discuss the matter.

I provided each teacher and head teacher with a copy of the synopsis of the second proposal, thus:

The use of objects in the education of children 3–5

I have already had to submit the proposal for funds from 1 October 1975 to 30 September 1977. Briefly, this is what I propose:
1. To spend the first year in three classrooms (the additional one being a reception class). During each term two of the classrooms would be studied.
2. Interviews with teachers and children on the basis of recordings would be attempted.
3. A check would be made as to whether there is progress in the use of objects in the classrooms. If this was so, a diagnostic checklist could be constructed for use by teachers to check on this progress.
4. A boy and a girl in each classroom would be recorded over two terms. This would establish the specific experiences within the

class as a whole. The class as a whole would occasionally be monitored, also through recording.

5. With permission, the teachers could see each other's recordings and give accounts, which would remain confidential.

6. Parents of the children being intensively studied could, if they were interested, see their child in the class and the parents' accounts would be collected – also confidentially.

7. It is hoped that after consultation with teachers and educationalists a large format book could be prepared which would present pictures, transcript, and commentary of child activities over time. A separate book might report the research aspects of the work. Overall I hope that, reported in this way, the findings will be of use to teachers and teacher trainers; perhaps to equipment manufacturers and to people concerned with child development in general.

The Social Science Research Council did not approve a full grant, but extended the research by six months; the approval being received on 14 July. I immediately wrote to the Assistant Education Officer and received a reply dated 18 August. In this he suggested:

I think you may find the reception class conditions for which you are looking at one of the following schools:

(List of five schools)

You may approach one or more of these schools in September, and you will then be able to make your own selection of location subject to the support of the Head. There has not been time to prepare the ground for you, and the Heads will not have prior knowledge of your project. They will all be much concerned with the reception of new children on the first day of term, but I would expect them to be able to offer you an appointment within the first week, and I hope this will give you sufficient time.

It may be useful to spell out to each Head who will be involved with your work next year the process which you and I agreed concerning the recording of individual children. You will remember that we agreed the following steps to be followed:

(a) To establish the agreement and support of the head for such recording;

(b) To obtain the agreement of the Chairman of Managers to this process as a matter of principle;

(c) For you to select the individual children;

(d) For the head and yourself to make a joint approach to the parents in order to give them a full explanation of what is involved; and

(e) To obtain parental agreement, after which the parents should be kept informed and should have the opportunity to see and to comment on the recorded material.

I know that you appreciate the delicacy of these situations and I look forward to hearing from you the results of your further work.

I visited the first of the schools on the list, having made informal enquiries among people working within the Education Authority, on 5 September, and on that day wrote to the Assistant Education Officer thus:

> Thank you very much for your letter. I have just returned from a meeting with the head of the first school on your list. She was very co-operative, introducing me to a reception class teacher and showing me round that part of the school.
>
> I have left the sheet with the research intentions with her and have informed her of the confidentiality arrangements that we agreed. She will see the Chairman of Managers at a scheduled meeting in the next two weeks.
>
> I will be visiting the school again to discuss the research possibilities with the reception class teacher next Tuesday.
>
> Thanks again for your help.

An application to the Social Science Research Council was submitted in September 1975, with this response from the Secretary of the Educational Research Board:

> 12 December 1975
>
> I am writing about the outcome of your most recent application to us. Although the proposal was recommended for award, it did not receive a sufficiently high priority to allow the award of funds in the present very difficult financial situation.

I wrote to the schools as follows:

> 6 January 1976
>
> As you know, the research that you have so kindly facilitated has been supported through funding from the Social Science Research Council. In September I was asked to resubmit a proposal to complete the research. I have since heard from the Research Council that 'although the proposal was recommended for award, it did not receive a sufficiently high priority to allow the award of funds in the present very difficult financial situation'. I am unhappy to have to leave the work, especially because you have been so co-operative and generous.

I do hope to write something more substantial than the required Research Report. Should something like a book emerge, I will produce it under the agreed conditions of confidentiality and anonymity that I have been working with up to now. I will send draft copies to you for your comments, deletions and alterations.

Having not received the grant, I have no further salary from March 31, so have necessarily taken another research job at Bulmershe College of Higher Education. I will be in to see you, maybe several times, before I leave. Thank you once again for all your help, kindness and encouragement.

I wrote to also to the Assistant Education Officer as follows:

6 January 1976

I regret that the Social Science Research Council, although recommending my Nursery Project application for an award, has no funds at present for Projects that they consider to be not of the highest priority. Needless to say, I am very disappointed – not only was I getting on very well with the teachers and children, but I felt that I was collecting some very useful and interesting information. I have to submit a final Report and will let you and the schools have a copy. Should a book emerge, the agreed conditions of confidentiality and anonymity would be maintained. I would make sure that draft copies would be sent to the schools for their perusal.

Necessarily I have had to take another job – at Bulmershe College of Higher Education.

I want to thank you very much for your help and concern with this research.

from whom I received this reply:

20 January 1976

Thank you very much for your letter. I share your disappointment at the nursery project application being unsuccessful. Apart from the intrinsic potential value of the work, I felt that a relationship of constructive co-operation was developing and I know that the teachers with whom you have been working will regret their loss of contact with you. We are sorry to lose you from East Anglia and send you all good wishes for success and enjoyment in your new post.

With all the uncertainty I sometimes had some difficulty justifying to myself my presence within the schools which drew on teachers' co-operation and willingness to spend additional time as an informant. However, I am sure that the teachers' frank and honest replies were allowed to emerge partially through the mutually agreed conditions under which the research was to be conducted. I am sure that triangulation and the involvement of the teacher as informant is dependent upon the researcher's integrity and adherence to the explicit agreement.

(Adelman, 1976, 91, 22–8)

The above may seem overly formal, and inappropriate in this context because of the complications caused by research council funding, but experience suggests that it may not be so unusual or idiosyncratic an account as the inexperienced may think. At the very least you should be prepared to enter into the kind of process recounted here should the need arise, and preferably before the event rather than afterwards, for by then damage may already have been done.

Summary

This chapter has examined in some detail what might appear to be a preliminary and not too important stage of research. In fact finding a research problem and finding a place to work on it empirically is a major concern and one too often left out or reduced to insignificance in standard textbooks.

In this chapter we have looked mainly at procedural aspects of the process. There are also other issues in terms of selecting appropriate research methods and conceptualizing problems which will be picked up again in the chapters that follow.

3 Methods: issues and problems

Some preliminary definitions

The terms 'method', 'technique' and even 'methodology' tend to be used interchangeably. In order to clarify what follows it is useful to restrict the use of the term 'methodology' to its strict meaning as denoting 'the logic of methods'. It is in this sense not strictly appropriate to refer to 'qualitative methodology' except when the intention is to refer to the relation between particular methods and their context of use. A 'methodology' should specify methods but only in order to justify their use for defined purposes in specified situations and circumstances. It is in this sense both a higher-level and more abstract term – concerned with issues of meta-method – and a more specific term in that its context of use requires elaboration and justification.

Between 'method' and 'technique' it is more difficult to draw a demarcation. Some people use the term 'method' to specify research recipes and use 'technique' to refer to the detailed practice of these strategies. Hence, observation, interviews and questionnaires would be methods, while check-lists, multiple choice questions and interaction analysis would be techniques. Others use the word 'technique' to describe strategies and 'methods' to refer to a rather more general level of discussion (hence, 'statistical methods' or 'research methods').

The distinction is obviously a difficult one to make and perhaps always arbitrary. Precise definition is not necessary so long as you realize that the terms are used somewhat loosely and that there is considerable variety of usage in different texts and in different discussions. Here I will try to restrict myself to using 'methods' more generally, and use 'technique' to describe research recipes.

Making appropriate selections

A key decision in any research project involves the selection of methods. It is a decision that is usually made early in the life of a project, and once made not easily reversed, though it may be enhanced by the later addition of supplementary methods.

In most textbook discussions it is assumed that the selection of methods is made on a rational basis. Given the research problem, what is the best way to set about creating relevant research data? In practice decisions are rarely so clearly defined as this implies. As we have seen in Chapter 2, 'research problems' do not often present themselves ready-made from educational practice. They have to be worked on, reformulated and worried over before they take on a conformation that makes them amenable to a research approach. Even at this stage where the problem is formulated in research terms and a research design can be created, the 'real' problem may not emerge with any clarity until the data appear and some preliminary interpretation is made. In this sense the strict logical progression which a rational approach suggests, and which often appears in texts on research in one form or another, is inappropriate (see diagram on p. 47).

Emphasising the sequence from problem formulation to empirical testing and then to explanation not only reduces the significance of the 'pre-world' of problem formulation, but as I have suggested does not allow for the fact that, in practice, the choice of particular methods may predate the existence of the research problem. Selection of methods may be an act of faith rather than a rational response to a clearly formulated problem.

The method may even be an intrinsic part of the problem, rather than extrinsic and disconnected from it. Just as recipes are not simply things that are done to food, but become concepts within which method and substance are compounded, so 'method' in research can become an intrinsic part of the project.

Research process 'by the book'

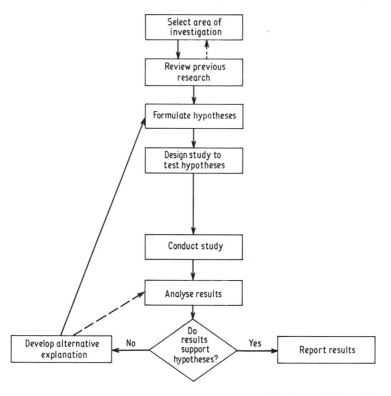

Source: Boehm, 1980, 496.

The methods we choose to use are, in this sense, there to be tested, just as much as the substantive hypotheses.

This is reinforced by the fact that we tend, as researchers, to favour some methods rather than others. Just as an instrument-alist will not change from playing the clarinet to playing the trumpet because a particular piece demands it, but will instead usually turn to another piece of music, searching for pieces that suit both the instrument and the player, so researchers generally give a lot of time and thought to the formulation of possible and potential research problems, looking for those that appear to fit their interests and preferred methods. Occasionally they will venture into new areas, but more often they will have a series of methods and approaches up their sleeves, some tried, some untried and awaiting testing. That methods go in search of problems is no surprise: it is after all the basis of most research in science, and it is in methods that most professional researchers vest their experience.

This presents particular problems for the applied researcher or evaluator who attempts to work at and from starting points and concerns presented by others outside the research community. In such cases it may be necessary to work with unfamiliar methods or with one where you lack expertise and

Summary of classroom research techniques

Method	Administration and equipment	Advantages
I Questionnaire	Outsider – Teacher Question sheet	1. Easy to administer. 2. Quick to fill in. 3. Relevance of questions. 4. Easy to follow up. 5. Provides direct comparison of groups and individuals.
II Questionnaire	Teacher – Child Question sheet	1. Feedback to teacher re: a) attitudes b) adequacy of resources c) assessment of adequacy of teacher help d) preparation for next session e) conclusions at end of term. 2. Quick to fill in. 3. As teacher is involved he is better able to effect and analyse questions. 4. Data are quantifiable.

are unsure of your judgement as to what can and cannot be done.

The following summary of various research methods is derived from the Ford Teaching Project. This project involved groups of teachers, who claimed in different ways to be using 'inquiry' and 'discovery' approaches to teaching, in doing research in their own classrooms. It is therefore a list compiled from the point of view of teachers wanting to research as well as teach, and so considers carefully the disadvantages of methods that are time consuming, demanding on the researcher or cumbersome to use.

Disadvantages	*Notes*
1. Time consuming analysis.	Relevant to groups rather than to individuals, i.e. data obtained from group of teachers. One questionnaire about one teacher irrelevant. Advantages point 5 – tells teacher about *other* teachers and *other* children. Outsider must always liaise closely with teacher.
2. Extensive preparation to get clear and relevant questions.	
3. Outsider must have clear object.	
4. Difficult to get questions that explore in depth – questionnaire may be very long.	
5. Who is suitable outsider?	
6. Suitable outsiders are difficult to obtain.	
1. As method above.	Anonymity encourages candour of replies but means individual problems cannot be followed up. Of direct use to classroom teacher – tells teacher of *own* class.
2. Effectiveness depends very much on reading ability and comprehension of the child.	
3. a) Children may be fearful of answering candidly.	
b) Children will try to produce 'right' answers.	

Method	Administration and equipment	Advantages
III Questionnaire	Outsider – Child Question sheet	1. As method II above. 2. Outsider is more likely to be unbiased.
IV Observation	Teacher – Self Whatever the individual prefers	1. No need for any special equipment or personnel. 2. Simple to administer over long periods. 3. Easy to isolate salient points. 4. Method does not interfere with teaching procedure.
V Observation	Outsider – Teacher Tape-recorder, notebook, camera, documents, or whatever the observer requires.	1. Lightens the teacher's problem of analysis of problems. 2. Observer will be more unbiased and objective. 3. A mobile observer can watch various teachers and may obtain good comparisons. 4. Observers can note and appreciate incidents that the teacher may miss.
VI Observation	Outsider – Child Tape-recorder ideal, activity list, inventory	1. Outsider can move freely and see all the children in different situations.

Disadvantages	*Notes*
1. As method II above	Outsider should consult teacher
2. Difficult for outsider to do any detailed follow-up work.	regarding contents of questionnaire.
3. Children can be put off by strangers.	
4. Availability of suitable outsider.	
1. Difficult to be fully objective.	See Research Technique 5, field
2. Can the teacher always see his own aims or faults?	notes. See 'A third-year form tries to
3. Need for a back-up system e.g. tape-recorder/notebook. This is time consuming.	enter a freer world: Research into ways towards Inquiry/Discovery working' a case study by Brian
4. Easy to pass things over in times of stress, e.g. 'I'll do this' then forget.	Iredale.
1. 'Spare' teachers or outsiders not easy to obtain.	
2. Observer must be briefed in advance on teacher's aims – time consuming.	
3. Observer must have a basic set of criteria on which to base his observations.	
4. How are the results processed? Discussions are time consuming. Written reports are time consuming and must be based on lengthy periods of observation to be of value.	
5. Observer must be continually present for lengthy periods to get full value of all occurrences. i.e. Little point being present first thing each day – routine soon established.	
6. Disadvantages of methods II and III.	
1. As in method V above.	See Ford Teaching Project
2. Children may be put off by tape-recorders.	Patterns of Teaching series: 'Three points of view in the
3. Virtually impossible for observer not to influence group's activity – curiosity value of outsider.	classroom', 'Self-monitoring questioning strategies', etc.

Method	Administration and equipment	Advantages
VII Tape-recorder	Teacher Cassette recorder	1. Very successfully monitors all conversations within range of the recorder. 2. Provides ample material with great ease. 3. Versatility – can be transported or left with a group. 4. Records personality developments. 5. Can trace development of group's activities.
VIII Tape-recorder	Outsider Cassette recorder or radio mike recorder	1. Very easy to administer. 2. Outsider has greater mobility than teacher and is better able to get to relevant situations. 3. Allows teacher to perform classroom routines. 4. Advantages of method VII above.
IX Slides in conjunction with tapes	Teacher Camera and accessories e.g. films, flashes, projector, tape-recorder, synchroniser carousel projector, radio mike	1. Some advantage may be obtained by looking at photographs of kids working, or at end products of their work, and as a stimulus for discussion. 2. As an instrument which helps you to get observation and comment from other teachers who were not present at the time. 3. See notes on tape-recording.

Disadvantages	Notes
1. Buying one!	Acclimatize children to presence
2. Nuisance to carry about (this can be overcome by radio mike).	of tape-recorder. Be selective over what is transcribed. Advantageous to have a battery-
3. Transcription largely prohibitive because of time involved.	operated cassette recorder with built-in microphone. See 'The Castles Group', a case
4. Masses of material may provide little of relevance.	study by Ken Forsyth.
5. Can disturb the children. Novelty. Can be inhibiting.	
6. Continuity can be disturbed by the practical problems of operating.	
7. Nothing visual – does not record silent activities.	
1. Follow-up with teacher means teacher must wade through pages of sometimes irrelevant material for the odd gem or listen to hours of recording.	Generally points for outsider are the same as for teacher.
2. As method VII above.	
1. Shows isolated situations. Difficulty of being in the right place at the right time. Concentrates on small groups and individuals; not classes.	
2. Slides may not truly depict activities of the children, i.e. photographer is selective.	
3. Can be a great distraction.	
4. Records nothing in depth. Shows nothing oral.	
5. Expense of capital outlay! Frequently superfluous; therefore costly.	
6. Equipment difficult to borrow.	
7. Film processing time can result in lengthy period between session being recorded and feedback to teacher.	
8. Requires operator.	

Method	Administration and equipment	Advantages
X Video TV	Cameraman Expensive photography and sound equipment plus skilled operator	1. Enables all situations to be constantly reviewed. 2. Origin of problems can be diagnosed. 3. Behavioural patterns of teacher and pupil can be seen. 4. Patterns of progress over long periods can be clearly charted.
XI Question analysis	Teacher – Child Question analysis sheet	1. Quick method of recording. 2. Questions ticked off as they arise; reduces writing to a minimum. 3. Simple and cheap. 4. Records happenings as they arise and at first hand. 5. Recording of questions neatly pigeon-holes problem areas in children's activities. 6. Will yield quantitative data.
XII Field notes	Teacher Field note-book	1. Very simple. No outsider needed at all. 2. Good on-going record. Used as a diary it gives good continuity. 3. First-hand information can be studied conveniently in teacher's own time. 4. Acts as an aide-memoire. 5. Helps to relate incidents, explore emerging trends, etc. 6. Very useful if teacher intends to write a case study.

Disadvantages	Notes
1. Extremely expensive to operate.	If required, make enquiries at local teachers' centre regarding availability.
2. Need for skilled technician to operate the equipment.	
3. Can be very conspicuous and distracting (see 7).	
4. Not generally available to teachers.	
5. If camera recording automatically, may record an empty frame.	
6. If camera directed by operator it will record only that which will be deemed to be of interest, i.e. operator acts as editor.	
7. Ethical problems relating to use of hidden cameras.	
1. Need to think up question categories in advance.	See Research Technique 4. See 'Team based action research', Ford Teaching Project case study
2. Vast number of possible happenings can mean that question analysis sheet is too long or too simplified for depth of detail.	
3. Even a simple sheet can need much work.	
4. If recording sheet can successfully discriminate between questions it may become too cumbersome, i.e. teacher may not be able to classify questions adequately in time available.	
1. Need to fall back on aids such as question analysis sheets, tapes and transcripts.	See Research Technique 5.
2. Conversation impossible to record by field notes.	
3. Notebook works with small groups but not with a full class. Initially time consuming.	
4. Can be highly subjective.	

Method	Administration and equipment	Advantages
XIII Standard assessment tests	Teacher – Child Tests	1. Very convenient. 2. Very standard. 3. Gives some information, e.g. maths ability, very clearly. 4. Simple to analyse.
XIV Interview	Teacher – Child Any means of recording as covered previously	1. Teacher in direct contact with child. 2. Child familiar, therefore more at ease. 3. Teacher can get to the root of problems. 4. Teacher able to seek information he wants directly and not through a ream of superfluous information. 5. Can work in lesson time or outside lesson time. 6. Can follow up problems immediately they arise and get information while minds are still fresh. 7. Good method of identifying individual's problems.
XV Interview	Outsider – Teacher Any means of recording as covered previously	1. Outsider can ask more objective questions. 2. Better able to foresee the problems (in some cases) that need investigating. 3. Discussion of ideas could lead on to further developments.

Disadvantages	*Notes*
1. Very limited scope – shows only intellectual ability and not the origin and solution of problems. 2. Unlikely to record much difference in the short term.	See 'The Castles Group', a case study by Ken Forsyth.
1. Time consuming, especially in long term. 2. May be carried out with some form of recording equipment, with attendant disadvantages. 3. Frequently difficult to get younger children to explain their thoughts and feelings.	See Research Technique 1. See Ford Teaching Project case studies. See Patterns of Teaching series.
1. This is only an aid in that feedback must still go to the teacher for action – may be time consuming. 2. As the research is into the work of a particular teacher or class, the aims of that teacher must be communicated to the outsider in advance so that he can base his interview along the right lines of enquiry. 3. For a successful study over a long period the interviewer has to be kept in touch with the work via direct observation or from direct information from the teacher – this may be time consuming. 4. Outsiders are difficult to obtain.	As above.

Method	Administration and equipment	Advantages
XVI Interview	Outsider – Child Any means of recording as covered previously	1. Leaves teacher free as the interviewer discovers initial information from the child. 2. Teacher is able to maintain his duties in class as outsider is doing the observing. 3. Child frequently more candid with outsider than with class teacher or teacher from within the school. 4. Outsider is likely to be more objective. 5. Outsider can focus information the child provides along predetermined lines of investigation.
XVII Case study	Teacher Any methods of acquiring information that are available to the teacher, i.e. the research methods and equipment outlined above	1. A relatively simple way of plotting the progress of a course of work, or a pupil's or group's reactions to teaching methods. 2. Information yielded by case studies will tend to give a more accurate and representative picture than will any one of the research methods detailed above, since they should draw on data gathered by as many of these methods as possible.

Disadvantages	Notes
1. Child unfamiliar, may be reluctant to divulge relevant information.	As above.
2. Mutual uncertainty.	
3. If the teacher is the primary agent in the research, then he will get his information second-hand and subject to the biases of the interviewer.	
4. The whole set-up is time consuming as information goes from child to interviewer to teacher.	
5. Difficulty in obtaining skilled outsider.	
1. In order for the case study to be of value it must be fairly exhaustive. This means that it will be time consuming in its preparation and its writing.	See Ford Teaching Project case studies. Ideally a case study should be composed from data that have been obtained from a great many sources. i.e. from many of the research methods already mentioned. The case study is, however, an agent of classroom research in its own right.
2. Feedback available to teacher only after considerable lapse of time.	

(Forsyth and Wood, n.d., 25–36)

The accumulation of this kind of practical knowledge provides an important background to decisions that need to be made concerning the selection of research methods when faced by particular research problems. The list of available methods needs extending, however, beyond the rather basic and conventional list that the Ford Teaching Project provides. Nick Smith, of the North West Regional Educational Laboratory in Oregon, has recently investigated a much wider range of possible sources for research and evaluation methods. The 'Research on Evaluation Program' has come up with an impressive and surprising range of possibilities. The catalogue of reports available from the project includes thirty–eight distinct and different methods ranging from those involving elaborate statistical techniques through to literary criticism and water–colour painting. A sample of the catalogue is given here as an illustration, including the full contents page and four examples of data collection and analysis strategies.

Revised catalog of method descriptions

Data collection and analysis strategies
    1. Assignment models
    2. Transportation models
    3. Dynamic programming
★ 4. Queueing theory
    5. Minimum–maximum goal projection
    6. Geocode analysis
★ 7. Trend surface analysis
    8. Social area analysis/ecological analysis
    9. Concept analysis
  10. Thematic matrix analysis
★11. Document analysis
  12. Legislative history
  13. The key interview
  14. Interviewing: circling, shuffling and filling
  15. Documenting files and summaries
  16. Cost-benefit analysis
  17. Cost-effectiveness analysis
★18. Cost-utility analysis
  19. Cost-feasibility analysis

Sampling strategies
  20. Blanket sampling
  21. Shadow sampling
  22. Time-based sampling
  23. Event-based sampling
  24. Dimensionally based sampling

Reporting strategies
  25. Research briefs
  26. Appeals procedures
  27. Storytelling
  28. Compelling the eye
  29. Representation of reality
  30. Accurate, sharp descriptions
  31. Graphic displays
  32. Stem and leaf displays and box plots
  33. Still photography
  34. Oral briefings
  35. Briefing panel presentations
  36. Adversary hearings
  37. Committee hearings
  38. Television presentations of hearings

* See following pages

Method Description Sheet 4

Method: Queueing theory.

Purpose: Queueing theory can be used to study waiting line problems.

Why and when to use: Queueing theory is used whenever there are delays in waiting lines. For example, students often wait in line at libraries, cafeterias, and showers. They also wait in line at the offices of school nurses, vice-principals, and counselors. One of two errors will often be present: either customers are waiting for service, or servers are waiting for customers. Most questions will center around three major questions: (1) How much of the time will the service channels (e.g. library checkout desk) be idle? (2) How many customers (e.g. students) will usually be waiting for service? (3) How long of a wait will each customer typically have?

Basic procedures: Mathematical models are fitted to aspects of queueing behavior. If arrivals are assumed to be random, the probability that there will be *no* student arriving at the service channel is an exponential function of the number of minutes elapsed since the last arrival. One key distribution that follows from this is called the Poisson distribution. From this information it is possible to derive formulas which give the probability of finding a service channel idle at any particular time, the probability of having a certain number of customers either being served or waiting in line, the mean queue length, the expected number of customers waiting for service, the expected waiting time of a new arrival, and the probability of having a waiting line longer than a certain number of customers.

Advantages/benefits: Using the measured information of the number of students arriving per minute, and the number of students serviced in a minute, it is possible to calculate a wide array of information about the queueing system which is useful for making decisions about it.

Disadvantages/costs: Within queueing theory there is no automatic answer. The theory does not lay out decision alternatives. For example, in the case of the library checkout desk, we might calculate the waiting time and decide that it is unacceptably large. Note that queueing theory does not help us make the decision of whether or not the waiting time is unacceptably long.

Resources required: None.

Basic references:

Eck, R. D. *Operations research for business.* Chapter 8. Belmont, CA: Wadsworth, 1976.

Hillier, F. S., & Lieberman, G. J. *Introduction to operations research.* Chapter 6. San Francisco: Holden-Day, 1967.

Page, E. B. *Educational evaluation through operations research.* No. 30 of the Paper and Report Series of the Research on Evaluation Program. Portland, Ore.: Northwest Regional Educational Laboratory, 1979.

Trueman, R. E. *An introduction to quantitative methods in decision making.* Chapter 8. New York: Holt, Rinehart and Winston, 1977.

Method Description Sheet 7

Method: Trend surface analysis.

Purpose: Trend surface analysis is a technique from geology used to generate three-dimensional contour maps on which to illustrate changes in important variables. Variations in a particular variable over a geographic region are partitioned into broad regional trends and small-scale local deviations from these trends.

Why and when to use: Trend surface analysis has been used to study the relationship between geographic location and the following: school board elections and sources of local school support; the dissemination of information on Title III projects; statewide educational needs assessment; factors such as personal income, educational background, unemployment, number of dependents and financial support for local education.

Basic procedures: 1. *Stations* are the points in the geographic region chosen to represent a local geographic area. For example, in a study of fourth grade IQ scores, each school would be a station and the average IQ at the fourth grade level would be the *station value*. 2. Each station is identified by three data points: x, y coordinates which establish the station's geographic location, and the station value for the variable of interest, the z coordinate. A statistical modelling procedure is employed (e.g., least squares polynomial trend fittings) and a surface equation is produced. 3. The surface equation can then be used to construct a contour map indicating regional trends and local trends. 4. Residuals can be computed and residual maps plotted to identify hidden trends and deviant stations. 5. Multiple surface maps can be overlayed to illustrate regional interactions between variables of interest.

Advantages/benefits: Trend surface analysis is a useful technique for the visual display of large amounts of data. Using computers and high-speed plotters, the evaluator can generate multiple data maps which portray geographic data relationships not discernible through tabular display.

Disadvantages/costs: The technique requires computer analysis and plotting facilities.

Resources required: A computer program and access to a computer with plotting facilities.

Basic references: The following provide general introduction to trend surface analysis:

Lewis, M. S. Trend surface analysis of community variables. *Psychological Bulletin*, 1977, 84, 940–949.

McIsaac, D. N. *The application of trend surface analysis.* Paper presented at the Annual Meeting of the American Educational Research Association, Chicago, Illinois, 1972. (ERIC Number ED 064 894)

McIsaac, D. N. *The people of the state: A description through trend surface analysis.* 1973. (ERIC Number ED 082 673)

McIsaac, D. N. Trend surface analysis. In H. J. Walberg (Ed.) *Evaluating educational performance.* Berkeley: McCutchan, 1974.

Smith, N.L. Techniques for the analysis of geographic data in evaluation. *Evaluation and Program Planning*, 1979, *2*, 119–126.

Method Description Sheet 11

Method: Document analysis.

Purpose: Document analysis is the analysis of documents in order to gather facts.

Why and when to use: Document analysis is superior in finding out retrospective information about a program, and may be the only way that certain information is available. Document analysis is particularly useful at the beginning of an evaluation when the evaluator is trying to understand why the program is the way it is. Documents are an excellent source for determining the purposes, rationale, and history of a program. Doing document analysis is usually a useful prelude to collecting new data. Knowing the purposes of a program helps the evaluator decide what data are to be collected. Doing document analysis one finds out when data have already been collected and what new data need to be collected.

Basic procedures: Tracking is a process of working through documents looking for information that will confirm some hypothesis. *Content analysis* is the creation of categories in order to analyse documents. *Case study aggregation* is a means for aggregating diverse case studies together using a common conceptual framework so that the findings will be cumulative.

Advantages/benefits 1. Document analysis is superior to interviewing for collecting some kinds of retrospective data. 2. Information obtained from documents is often more credible than information obtained via observation and interviewing. 3. Documents are convenient to use. 4. Documents are often available free or at little cost. 5. Documents are non-reactive: that is, it is not usual to find masking or sensitivity because the producer knows he or she is being studied by some social scientist. 6. Records save the time and money that original data collection requires. 7. Program documents provide the evaluator with information about many things that cannot be observed because they may have taken place before the evaluation was begun and because they may include private interchanges to which the evaluator is not directly privy.

Disadvantages/costs: 1. Often, documents are written to make a program look good and thus can be misleading. 2. There is a dependency on the memory of the person doing the reporting. 3. Although reams of material may be available, it often will not contain much of the needed information or be sufficiently detailed. 4. Documents may reflect clerical lapses, typographical errors, biases, or outright deception. 5. Agency records may be inaccurate, out of date, or months behind on entries. 6. The definitions and categories used by an agency's records may be inappropriate for evaluation purposes. 7. Documentary facts never come 'pure', since they are always refracted through the mind of the recorder. 8. Documents may provide unrepresentative samples.

Resources required: None:

Basic references:

Caulley, D. N. *Document analysis in program evaluation.* No. 60 of the Paper and Report Series of the Research on Evaluation Program. Portland,Ore.: Northwest Regional Educational Laboratory, 1981.

Guba, E. G. Investigative reporting. In N. L. Smith (Ed.), *Metaphors for evaluation: Sources of new methods.* Beverly Hills: SAGE Publications, 1981.

Guba, E. G., and Lincoln, Y. S. *Effective evaluation.* San Francisco: Jossey-Bass, 1981.

Murphy, J. T. *Getting the facts.* Santa Monica: Goodyear, 1980.

Method Description Sheet 18

Method: Cost-utility analysis.

Purpose: To compare the costs and benefits to society of various policy alternatives.

When and why to use: When benefits cannot be measured in monetary terms or in terms of effectiveness, cost utility is the alternative. When subjective assessment must be made about the nature and probability of educational benefits as well as their relative worth, cost-utility analysis may be an appropriate tool.

Basic procedures: First, the decision maker uses the information available to him or her to ascertain the probability of achieving particular educational outcomes with each of the policy alternatives. With the cost-utility approach there can be more than one outcome per alternative. Second, the decision maker places relative values on each of the educational outcomes to weight them according to their desirability. The method for doing this is to rate each potential outcome on a scale of utility which reflects the desirability of that outcome. For example, a decision maker could assess the value of each outcome on a $0-10$ point scale with equal intervals, in which 10 represents the highest value. Third, the subjective probability of each outcome is multiplied by the utility placed upon the outcome and adding these products across outcomes. This calculation is done separately for each policy alternative. Finally, costs are divided by the expected utilities to obtain cost-utility ratios for each alternative.

Advantages/benefits: Cost-utility analysis permits the use of a wide range of types of both qualitative and quantitative data in forming the decision. The advantages of the cost-utility approach are that the data requirements are less stringent than cost-benefit or cost-effectiveness approaches, that a large number of potential outcomes can be included in the evaluation, and that imperfect information and uncertainty can be addressed systematically.

Disadvantages/costs: The highly subjective nature of the assessments of effectiveness and the values placed upon them by the decision maker prevents the kind of replicability from analysis-to-analysis that might be obtained with the more stringent cost-benefit and cost-effectiveness approaches.

Resources required: None.

Basic references:

Edwards, W., Guttentag, M., & Snapper, K. A decision-theoretic approach to evaluation research. In E. L. Struening and M. Guttentag, (Eds.), *Handbook of evaluation research*, Vol. 1. Beverly Hills: SAGE Publications, 1975.

Stokey, E., & Zeckhauser, R. *A primer for policy analysis.* New York: W. W. Norton & Co., 1978.

Levin, H. M. *Casebook on cost analysis in educational evaluation* (No. 33 of the Paper and Report Series of the Research on Evaluation Program). Portland, Ore: Northwest Regional Educational Laboratory, 1979.

(Gray *et al.*, 1983, 25, 30, 33, 37, 44)

Given the increasing number of available methods it is important to emphasize that the issue is not simply one of matching methods to presenting problems. As we have seen, before this occurs it is necessary to work hard on the definition and formulation of the problem itself. This is particularly important when problems or tasks are commissioned, for it is often the case that the problem or task presented (like the symptoms revealed to the doctor) are not those that most concern the person or people involved. When a school says it faces communication difficulties, or that it has problems with a particular group of children, or with an area of the curriculum, this often indicates (or obscures) a more serious worry. Indeed the researcher may have to judge, in the light of little familiarity with or understanding of the circumstances, whether to take on the task as presented or whether to probe beyond it. Subtle diagnosis may be needed before decisions are made about pre-scribing a course of treatment. This in turn puts stress on the researcher to know what can and cannot be done with particular methods, and what unintended outcomes may result from using them. A method that in technical respects is ideal may be unusable if it takes too long or if it creates anxiety and conflict in the school.

For the most part it is difficult to gain access to the pre-world of applied research; that is, to the stage of negotiating the initial formulation of the study. The American evaluator Bob Stake has, however, encapsulated some of his accumulated wisdom in the form of a dialogue with a potential client. It is included here in full.

A conversation between a person who will commission an evaluation study and an evaluation specialist favouring a responsive approach

C: As I said in my letter I have asked you to stop by because we need an evaluator for our National Experimental Teaching Programme. You have been recommended very highly. But I know you are very busy.

E: I was pleased to come in. The new Programme is based on some interesting ideas and I hope that many teachers will benefit from your work. Whether or not I personally can and should be involved remains to be seen. Let's not rule out the possibility. There might be reasons for me to set aside other obligations to be of help here.

C: Excellent. Did you have a chance to look over the programme materials I sent you?

E: Yes, and by coincidence, I talked with one of your field supervisors, Mrs Bates. We met at a party last week. She is quite enthusiastic about the plans for group problem-solving activities.

C: That is one thing we need evaluation help with. What kind of instruments are available to assess problem-solving? Given the budget we have, should we try to develop our own tests?

E: Perhaps so. It is too early for me to tell. I do not know enough about the situation. One thing I like to do is to get quite familiar with the teaching and learning situations, and with what other people want to know, before choosing tests or developing new ones. Sometimes it turns out that we cannot afford or cannot expect to get useful information from student performance measures.

C: But surely we shall need to provide some kind of proof that the students are learning more, or are understanding better, than they did before! Otherwise how can we prove the change is worthwhile? We do have obligations to evaluate this programme.

E: Perhaps you should tell me a little about those obligations.

C: Yes. Well, as you know, we are under some pressure from the Secretary (of Health, Education and Welfare), from Members of Congress, and the newspapers. They have been calling for a documentation of 'results'.

But just as important, we in this office want to know what our programme is accomplishing. We feel we cannot make the best decisions on the amount of feedback we have been getting.

E: Are there other audiences for information about the National Experimental Teaching Programme?

C: We expect others to be interested.

E: Is it reasonable to conclude that these different 'audiences' will differ in what they consider important questions, and perhaps even what they would consider credible evidence?

C: Yes, the researchers will want rigor, the politicians will want evidence that the costs can be reduced, and the parents of students will want to know it helps their children on the College Board Examinations. I think they would agree that it takes a person of your expertise to do the evaluation.

E: And I will look to them, and other important constituencies, teachers and taxpayers, for example, to help identify pressing concerns and to choose kinds of evidence to gather.

C: Do you anticipate we are going to have trouble?

E: Of course, I anticipate some problems in the programme. I think the evaluator should check out the concerns that key people have.

C: I think we must try to avoid personalities and stick to objective data.

E: Yes, I agree. And shouldn't we find out which data will be considered relevant to people who care about this programme? And some of the most important facts may be facts about the problems people are having with the programme. Sometimes it does get personal.

C: The personal problems are not our business. It is important to stick to the impersonal, the 'hard-headed' questions, like 'How much is it costing?' and 'How much are the students learning?'

E: To answer those questions effectively I believe we must study the programme, and the communities, and the decision-makers who will get our information. I want any evaluation study I work on to be useful. And I do not know ahead of time that the cost and achievement information I could gather would be useful.

C: I think we know what the funding agencies want: information on cost and effect.

E: We could give them simple statements of cost, and ignore such costs as extra work, lower morale, and opportunity costs. We could give them gain scores on tests, and ignore what the tests do not measure. We know that cost and effect information is often superficial, sometimes even misleading. I think we have an obligation to describe the complexities of the programme, including what it is costing and what its results appear to be. And I think we have an obligation to say that we cannot measure these important things as well as people think we can.

C: Well, surely you can be a little less vague as to what you would do. We have been asked to present an evaluation design by a week from next Wednesday. And if we are going to have any pre-testing this year we need to get at it next month.

E: I am not trying to be evasive. I prefer gradually developed plans – 'progressive focusing' Partlett and Hamilton call it. I would not feel pressed by the deadline. I would perhaps present a sketch like this one (drawing some papers from a folder); one which Les McLean used in the evaluation of an instant-access film facility. His early emphasis was on finding out what issues most concern the people in and around the project.

C: I think of that as the Programme Director's job.

E: Yes, and the evaluation study might be thought of – in part – as helping the Programme Director with his job.

C: Hmmm. It is the Secretary I was thinking we would be helping. You made the point that different people need different information, but it seems to me that you are avoiding the information that the Secretary and many other people want.

E: Let's talk a bit about what the Secretary, or any responsible official, wants. I am not going to presume that a cost–effectiveness ratio is what he wants, or what he would find useful. We may decide later that it is.

First of all, I think that what a responsible official wants in this situation is evidence that the National Programme people are carrying out their contract, that the responsibility for developing new teaching techniques continues to be well placed, and that objectionable departures from the norms of professional work are not occurring.

Second, I think a responsible official wants information that can be used in discussions about policy and tactics.

Our evaluation methodology is not refined enough to give cost-effectiveness statements that policy-setters or managers can use. The conditionality of our ratios and our projections is formidable. What we can do is acquaint decision-makers with this particular programme, with its activities and its statistics, in a way that permits them to relate it to their experiences with other programmes. We do not have the competence to manage educational programmes by ratios and projections – management is still an art. Maybe it should remain an art – but for the time being we must accept it as a highly particularized and judgmental art.

C: I agree – in part. Many evaluation studies are too enormously detailed for effective use by decision-makers. Many of the variables they use are simplistic, even though they show us how their variables correlate with less simplistic measures. Some studies ignore the unrealistic arrangements that are made as experimental controls. But those objectionable features do not make it right to de-emphasize measurement. The fact that management is an art does not mean that managers should avoid good technical information.

What I want from an evaluation is a good reading – using the best techniques available – a good reading of the principal costs and of the principal benefits. I have no doubt that the evaluation methodology we have now is sufficient for us to show people in government, in the schools, and in the general public what the programme has accomplished.

E: If I were to be your evaluator I would get you that reading. I would use the best measures of resource allocation, and of teaching effort, and of student problem-solving we can find. But I would be honest in reporting the limitations of those measures. And I would find other ways also of observing and reporting the accomplishments and the problems of the National Programme.

C: That of course is fair. I do not want to avoid whatever real problems there may be. I do want to avoid collecting opinions as to what problems (and accomplishments) there might be. I want good data. I want neither balderdash nor gossip. I want my questions answered and I want the Secretary's questions answered.

And those questions might change as we go along. You would call that 'formative evaluation'?

E: Sometimes. I would also call it 'responsive'.

C: What kind of final report would you prepare for us?

E: I brought along couple of examples of previous reports. I can leave them with you. I can provide other examples if you would like. Whether there is a comprehensive or brief final report, whether there is one or several, those decisions can be made later.

C: No, I'm afraid that simply won't do. If we are to commit funds to an evaluation study, we must have a clear idea in advance of how long it is going to take, what it will cost, and what kind of product to expect. That does not mean that we could not change our agreement later.

E: If you need a promise at the outset, we can make it. Believe me, I do not believe it is in your best interests to put a lot of specifications into the 'contract'. I would urge you to choose your evaluator in terms of how well he has satisfied his previous clients more than on the promises he would make so early.

C: It would be irresponsible of me not to have a commitment from him.

E: Of course. And your evaluator should take some of the initiative in proposing what should be specified and what options should be left open.

C: Let me be frank about one worry I have. I am afraid I may get an evaluator who is going to use our funding to 'piggy-back' a research project he has been wanting to do. He might agree to do 'our' evaluation study but it might have very little to do with the key decisions of the Experimental Teaching Programme.

E: It is reasonable to expect any investigator to continue old interests in new surroundings. When you buy him you buy his curiosities. He may develop hypotheses, for example, about problem solving and teaching style, hypotheses that sound most relevant to the programme – but the test of these hypotheses may be of little use to those who sponsor, operate, or benefit from the programme.

His favourite tactics, a carefully controlled comparative research effort or a historical longitudinal research study, for example, might be attractive to your staff. But he is not inclined to talk about how unnecessary this approach may be. The inertia in his past work may be too strong. You are right, there is a danger. I think it can best be handled by looking at the assignments the evaluator has had before, and by getting him to say carefully what he is doing and why, and by the sponsor saying very carefully which he wants and does not want, and by everybody being sceptical as to the value of each undertaking, and suggesting alternatives.

C: Would you anticipate publishing the evaluation study in a professional journal?

E: Even when an article or book is desired it is rare for an evaluation study to be suitable for the professional market. Evaluation studies are too long, too multi-purposive, too non-generalizable and too dull for most editors. Research activities within the evaluation project sometimes are suitable for an audience of researchers.

I usually suppose that my evaluation work is not done for that purpose. If something worth publishing became apparent I would talk over the possibilities with you.

C: I think something like that should be in writing. What other assurances can you give me that you would not take advantage of us? Do you operate with some specific 'rules of confidentiality'?

E: I would have no objection to a contract saying that I would not release findings about the project without your authorization. I consider the teachers, administrators, parents and children also have rights here. Sometimes I will want to get a formal release from them. Sometimes I will rely on my judgment as to what should and should not be made public, or even passed along to you. In most regards I would follow your wishes. If I should find that you are a scoundrel, and it is relevant to my evaluation studies, I will break my contract and pass the word along to those whom I believe should know.

C: I have nothing to lose, but others involved may have. I do not want to sanction scurrilous muck-raking in the name of independent evaluation. I wonder if you are too ready to depend on your own judgment. What if it is you who are the scoundrel?

E: I would expect you to expose me.

C: By exposing you I would be exposing my bad judgment in selecting you – the line of thought I would return to is the safeguard you would offer us against mismanagement of the evaluation study.

E: The main safeguard, I think, is what I was offering at the beginning: communication and negotiation. In day to day matters I make many decisions, but not alone. My colleagues, my sponsors, my information sources help make those decisions. A good contract helps, but it should leave room for new responsibilities to be exercised. It should help assure us that we will get together frequently and talk about what the evaluation study is doing and what it should be doing.

C: What about your quickness to look for problems in the programme? Perhaps you consider your own judgment a bit too precious.

E: I do not think so. Perhaps. I try to get confirmation from those I work with and from those who see things very differently than I do. I deliberately look for disconfirmation of the judgments I make and the judgments I gather from others. If you are thinking about the judgments of what is bad teaching and learning, I try to gather the judgments of people both who are more expert than I and those who have a greater stake in it than I. I cannot help but show some of my judgments, but I will look for hard data that support my judgment and I will look just as hard for evidence that runs counter to my opinion.

C: That was nicely said. I did not mean to be rude.

E: You speak of a problem that cuts deeply. There are few dependable checks on an evaluator's judgment. I recognise that.

C: You would use consultation with the project staff and with me, as a form of check and balance.

E: Yes. And I think that you would feel assured by the demands I place upon myself for corroboration and cross-examination of findings.

C: Well, there seems to me to be a gap in the middle. You have talked about how we would look for problems and how you would treat findings – but will there be any findings? What will the study yield?

E: If I were to be your evaluator we might start by identifying some of the key aims, issues, arrangements, activities, people, etc. We would ask ourselves what decisions are forthcoming, what inform-ation would we like to have. I would check these ideas with the programme staff. I would ask you and them to look over some things I and other evaluators have done in the past, and say what looks worth doing. The problem would soon be too big a middle, and we would have to start our diet.

C: I don't care much for the metaphor.

E: That may be as good a basis as any for rejecting an evaluator – his bad choice of metaphors.

C: I've just realized how late it is. I am hoping not to be rejecting any evaluators today. Perhaps you would be willing to continue this later.

E: Let me make a proposal. I appreciate the immediacy of the situation. I know a young woman with a doctorate and research experience, who might be available to co-ordinate the evaluation work. If so, I could probably be persuaded to be the director, on a quarter-time basis. Let me go over your materials with her. We would prepare a sketch of an evaluation plan, and show it to you along with some examples of her previous work.

C: That is a nice offer. Let me look at your examples and think about it before you go ahead. Would it be all right if I called you first thing tomorrow morning? Good. Thanks very much for coming by.

Commentary on the conversation with a responsive evaluator

I recognised as I started to develop this conversation that the negotiating conditions that I had experienced and the rhetoric I was familiar with were not common in other countries. I felt that the tenacious reader could overcome those parochial features to get at issues that are common to evaluation of large-scale programmes anywhere.

Many readers would prefer a listing of issues rather than a dialogue; I agree that listings can be helpful. I do believe that issues take on a different meaning when they are presented in natural discourse, and that it is useful for practitioners and theorists alike to give attention to these different meanings. The interweaving of pride, vulnerability, aspiration, and other personal and political characteristics into educational purpose and method are more apparent in such discourse than in such a checklist. . . .

I wanted to keep it a two-person, informal situation for simplicity and because I guessed that that would be most common in Europe. In the USA open bidding for evaluation contracts is required by law for many national and state programmes. The negotiations have become formal, legalistic, often impersonal, with little attention to the issues raised in this dialogue. Since I was too unfamiliar with any European setting and frame of mind I kept the idea of a conversation but made it an American scenario.

I sent an early draft of this conversation to the following persons for comments, particularly as to how the Commissioner might respond:

Heinrich Bauersfeld
Mathematics Curriculum Developer
University of Bielefeld

Joseph M. Cronin
Secretary of Educational Affairs
State of Massachusetts

Astrid Nyström
National Board of Education
Stockholm

Nils-Eric Svensson,
Executive Director
Stiftelsen Riksbankens Jubileumsfond
Stockholm

R. A. Becher
Nuffield Foundation
London

Robert Glasser, Co-Director
Learning Research and Development Center
University of Pittsburgh

Lawrence Stenhouse, Director
Centre for Applied Research in Education
University of East Anglia

Marc Tucker
National Institute of Education
Washington, DC

Most of these respondents found the issues relevant and difficult to resolve. Most noted the discrepancies between their real situations and the fictitious situation. I used many of the wordings they suggested in revising the dialogue. Most of them wanted a quicker declaration of purposes and plans, but my responsive evaluator is convinced that many of the shortcomings of evaluation studies are traced to a willingness to guess at what the key variables and issues are and to make an irretrievable commitment to personnel and instrumentation. And so he is vague, but explorative; anxious to base his worthiness on past performance rather than on what he might promise at present. It is not a stance that all the respondents found persuasive. Some of the reactions of the eight administrators named above are most insightful. I quote a sample of these reactions:

> 'Now, if this were my country the project leader would probably not be so free to make his own decisions. They would have been made at a "higher" level.'
>
> 'Over here a project director has to fight to get his project evaluated.'
>
> '. . . how clearly this conversation brought out the differing assumptions made in the US from those which would be made in this country – for example, that funds are normally made available under contract, that such contracts stipulate the need for evaluation, and that they impose tight deadlines.'
>
> 'The dialogue presupposes that the evaluator is a well-known person. . . . A minor researcher, on his way up . . . might expect to be treated with more firmness and prejudice by the commissioner.'
>
> 'I read your hypothetical conversation over and over again, and [I found the evaluator] too damn patronizing.'
>
> 'It is necessary to clarify the project philosophy. What really shall be improved? . . . the teaching of fractions, the sensitivity of the teacher, the degree of variety/differentiatedness, the style of inter-action between teacher and students, or what else?'
>
> 'It should be more "product"-oriented, a typical concern of action administrators.'

'The commissioner might probe more to find out if the evaluator is really sympathetic to the programme, shares the values of the creators, thinks it has promise, is willing to concentrate on the goals and variables important to the project staff, shares with the project staff some agreement as to what might be valid indicators of project success.'

'Many commissioners would [want] the evaluator to present results . . . which go along with [their] own interests, or those of the decision makers at higher levels. The commissioner might discard the evaluator as soon as he realizes that the desired results cannot be bought so easily.'

'I would have had the commissioner more tough-minded . . . raising questions about time span, costs, and scope of the evaluation; the experience and qualifications of the evaluator; the "subjectivity" of the proposed evidence; the apparent untidiness of the evaluation design, and whether the evaluator's report will offer recommendations about the continuance or discontinuance of the experiment.'

'The commissioner might press for what the evaluator means by "usefulness" . . . is it the furtherance of science, of psychological methods, of parent insight, of the manipulative power of steering board members, of the child's self awareness, of . . .? If the evaluator tries to serve all these needs, he is overburdened and soon will become a distractor and an explosive power in the project.'

'The point is: How much do the commissioner and evaluator join the common insincerity of producing designs to which they do not stand by?'

'The commissioner might well want to know how much time of how many people with what kind of experience and training will be required, and at what cost.'

'Recognition should be made of the fact that commissioners do have particular constituencies and that a wise evaluation would help meet the questions of these constituencies, at the same time getting on with the problems that may lie deeper.'

'The commissioner might want to know whether the evaluator's preliminary observations will be available to project staff as the project proceeds, whether such views will be available to others, and what control he will have over *premature* release of findings.'

'The commissioner might want some "right of reply" to negative findings, whenever they are released, or a chance to confer with the evaluator on the basis of draft reports before the final reports are published.'

'The commissioner might want to know how disruptive the

evaluator will be, how much time of project staff he will take, whether he can make use of measures routinely administered, whether he will demand the use of control groups, etc.'

'If the evaluator's racial, ethnic, or cultural background are different from staff and students, the commissioner might try to find out if the evaluator sees those differences as a problem, and, if so, what the evaluator would propose to do about it.'

'Is it not too egotistical to "learn as much as we can from the project"? Such an outcome is the byproduct of the project, too often the only worthwhile one. A foundation will hardly pay millions for the learnings of the project staff and evaluators.'

'I would have suggested some additional issues, such as that of access to participating schools; information about the project's underlying aims; the right to confidentiality of participants in the programme, and the concern for "proof", rather than evidence, of success or failure.'

'I don't think our evaluators have audiences. They have to create them.'

Most of these respondents felt that more should have been accomplished in that hypothetical meeting of commissioner and evaluator. Most thought that it was realistic and included some of the more important issues that need to be resolved in such a negotiation.

(Stake, 1976, 68–77)

What Stake calls 'responsive evaluation' is sometimes taken to imply a relatively passive role for the evaluator, even a denial of responsibility. This example, however, reveals a dialogue of an educational kind with the evaluator in a teaching role. While the presenting problem provides a starting point and a constant reference, the evaluator's task is one of analysis and clarification in order to reach a realizable and useful design. Cynically this might be interpreted as talking the birds out of the trees, for the persuasive evaluator might be seen as drawing the discussion onto his or her own ground. Once the dialogue is established in research or evaluation territory the element of 'responsiveness' could be only cosmetic.

While it is true that evaluators can operate in this way, and can come to relish challenges to their salesmanship, it is, at the end of the day, in their interest to ensure that they restrict their role to a relatively technical level. After all, if they run away with the dialogue they risk losing the motivation and commitment of those they seek to serve.

Presenting problems are not always to be left un-discussed or un-negotiated. There are cases where they may be taken at face value – they may actually be the best places to begin research and be clear statements of a researchable kind, or they may best be considered so initially in order to develop a confident relationship between researcher and subject/client. Generally, however, it is more productive to take presenting problems as marking the starting point of a dialogue, and as a series of boundary constraints on that dialogue rather than as strict contractual limits.

This point in itself may need to be approached with caution and discussed with those involved. One researcher reports finding that this became an issue with those responsible for overseeing the project he was responsible for carrying out. Clem Adelman, in a study of student choice in Colleges of Higher Education commissioned by the DES, reported that:

The DES permanent civil servant considered that a study funded by the DES should adhere to the propositions of the original proposal. As the DES funded the study, they assumed the right to require that the enquiry followed these original specifications. Her Majesty's Inspectorate representatives, however were more concerned about allowing the project to maintain its 'academic freedom' and to develop according to the sort of information that was being collected, although adhering to a considerable extent to the 'spirit' of the original proposal.

(Adelman, 1979, 9–10)

While Stake's dialogue took place at a high level in the system it is one that is likely to be replicated at any level on which the researcher chooses to operate. Relationships with a school, a classroom or teacher or with an Authority are likely to lead to the same tension between providing a clear and unambiguous design at the contract stage, and a sure knowledge that as the research progresses this initial design will come to seem inadequate.

The problem the researcher faces is that it is in the early stage of the research that people are most likely to demand answers to questions of a specific kind about the intent, purpose, scope and use of the research, and rightly so. Yet this is the very point at which the researcher can be least confident and least sure of the answers that he or she gives. In such circumstances honesty can be less than reassuring, while glib but confident answers are likely to ring a false note and be remembered. It is of course easier to overcome these problems with people who have been involved in similar ventures in the past, though Adelman's account would suggest that experience has limited transferability.

All this points to the crucial significance of the early period of the research during which access is negotiated and the research problem/area/issue clarified. We have seen in Chapter 2 how crucial are the procedural aspects of this process, but we did not examine closely what the implications might be for the content and conception of the research. What I am suggesting here is that the 'pre-active' stage of research is also important in helping to clarify the task. Much of this stage is likely to involve discussion of methods and techniques, though not exclusively so. In the terms I defined at the start of the chapter it is primarily discussion of a methodological kind. One of the things it takes time to learn, and which often frustrates those with little experience of doing research, is how important this apparently unproductive phase is. It is often seen as being wasted time, delay, and generally a frustrating period to be got over as soon as possible. It is also a time when major and often irreversible decisions are taken, though they may not be recognized as such until much later.

Multiple methods, triangulations and triads

While the next chapter describes individual methods and techniques as though they represented a menu of either/or choices, it is important to consider ways in which these might be mixed and interrelated. Indeed in many projects the most significant findings have emerged from points at which different methods have complemented each other. For example, in a recent study of bilingual education (MacDonald and Kushner, 1983) an attempt was made to study issues inside one school by means of participant observation, and in the arena of city politics and educational administration through a series of interviews. The choice of methods, participant observation within the school and interviewing outside it, was used to search for continuities across a natural divide within the system.

In a rather different field, a fascinating study by Robert Faulkner has looked at the occupation of the freelance composer of musical film scores in Hollywood (Faulkner, 1982). Faulkner began with a series of interviews with composers which provided him with an initial understanding. (Strictly speaking this is inaccurate, since, as a musician himself, Faulkner already had an initial understanding from the inside.) While the interviews provided him with an interesting set of data, this raised a number of questions that needed pursuing further. In particular the composers talked about their relationships with producers and directors, who in terms of the process of film-making come together in the editing rooms at the point where the music is dubbed on to the sound track of the film. Faulkner found he had to switch to an observational mode of research in order to look more closely at the nature of this collaboration, which had come to his notice through the interviews. Later he had to return again to interviewing when he found that a statistical and documentary study of film credits led him to certain interpretations about the 'market' for composers in the film industry. This set of interviews was rather different from the first set, for instead of attempting to see the occupation from a subjective viewpoint, he was trying out interpretations that had arisen from observation and analysis.

The subject of this study might seem obscure to the educational researcher, but the principle of working from a number of different methods and interrelating them, which Faulkner calls a 'triad', is an important one that is often appropriate in educational investigations. Faulkner describes it generally:

A triad mode of data collection involves carrying out a sequential, step-by-step testing and discovery of ideas, hunches, hypotheses. The imagery is one of a loosely linked, interdependent set of strategies. It involves, of course, the selection and explicit definition of research problems, concepts, and indices. It involves frequent checking on the distribution of phenomena – an explicit parameter estimation operation. It also involves the development of provisional hypotheses and a controlled but relaxed (and ecumenical) approach to nailing down the relationship among variables. Multiples in data collection – a triad of, for instance, *observation, interviewing,* and *archives* or records – stimulate (one hopes) complexity and subtlety of insight. A Triad advocates a distinctive stance toward qualitative and quantitative information, namely, that it takes multiples and complexity in the data collection to capture and preserve multiples in the phenomenon of interest (i.e., industries, organizations, careers). A taste for improvisation in the simultaneous use of a Triad may keep one's enthusiasms pitched at moderate to high levels, may overcome defensiveness toward any single mode of data collection, may increase playfulness with respect to the object of study, may boost estimates of error contained in any single source of data, may cross-validate measures of the phenomenon, and may break the singular focus toward a problem that often accompanies monomethod research.

My enthusiasm for multimethod inquiry was acquired during my study of career development in this high performance industry. [Hollywood film score composers.] The strategic strengths and advantages of multimethod inquiry stand on three legs that I have called a Triad. Each leg represents a unique mode of data collection: one from interviews with both informants and respondents; the second from observation of people at work; and the third from documents, records and archives of the organization or industry in question. Each leg presents the researcher with a different vantage point. While it may be useful to focus extensive time and energy on one mode, the advantages of moving sequentially across all three are formidable.   (Faulkner, 1982, 80–1)

A similar example of multiple methods being used, but in educational research, comes from a study I carried out into the work of school inspectors (Walker, 1982). Like Faulkner I began by observing inspectors at work, travelling with them on 'typical days' and writing up descriptive accounts of 'a day in the life' kind. These I gave back to the people concerned and their responses provided the basis for interviews. At a later date they would often ask me to observe them on particular visits because they wanted a third person account. ('I'm going to a school next week that really puzzles me; why don't you come along?' or, 'I am not sure about my relationship with the head of F—— School; if you came too you could tell me what you thought.') Such initiatives provided the focus for a visit that might or might not prove to be the focus of part of the research, but it lent a purpose and provided an intention which allowed the research to proceed in a more focused fashion.

Faulkner would perhaps reserve the term 'triad' for cases where there is a degree of separation between the methods used; the term more commonly used for the close intercutting between methods is 'triangulation'. Triangulation was advocated by Webb *et al.* (1966) in their often quoted book *Unobtrusive Measures*. Like Faulkner they saw the use of multiple methods as providing a basis for research in which the whole was stronger than the sum of the parts. By combining methods to a single purpose it was possible to observe the same events from several points of view – to 'triangulate' in order to fix more accurately a position. Triangulation was used by the Ford Teaching Project, mentioned earlier, in the more specific sense of looking at classroom events from the three points of view of the observer, the teacher and the children. The Ford T booklets, *Three Points of View in the Classroom* and *The Tins*, describe and illustrate the approach in more detail.

The 'triangulation' approach developed by Ford T begins to do something rather different from the kind of triangulation advocated by Webb *et al.* Their formulation was based on positivist assumptions and in the accounts they give it is clear that the reality that concerns them is seen as existing outside the observer and the methods. In Ford T you begin to get a more phenomenological perspective, for in the triangulations they present the 'reality' comes to be seen as located in the different perceptions and suppositions of teachers, pupils and observers. The events are still there, but the paradoxes and ambiguities that arise between different points of view are less easily arbitrated or resolved. It is an approach that begins to take on some of the characteristics of the analyses of the families of schizophrenic adolescents 'treated' by R.D. Laing and his colleagues (see, for instance, Esterson, 1970). In these studies, which proceed through multiple interviews with different members of the family in various combinations with each other, the 'schizophrenia' ascribed to the 'patient' is seen as a response to a situation which contains within it essential contradictions. The person who finds herself at the centre of very different perceptions and views, and is faced with organizing them into a reality, can only do so, it is argued, by moving outside what is considered 'normal' behaviour. The triangulation approach is therefore reversed, for instead of looking at one fixed reality from various points in order to describe it more fully, the aim instead is to start from the central event (or person) and to look outwards at the very different perspectives that create its context.

Participant observation and action research

The power of multiple methods flexibly used should not be underestimated. What might at first sight appear to be not very rigorous methods, such as the open interview and unstructured observation, become much more powerful when used in conjunction with each other. Indeed part of the recent enthusiasm for qualitative methods in educational research stems more from their flexibility than from any other intrinsic merit they possess; for, unlike most quantitative methods, they can be adapted and changed as a project progresses.

It is important to mention participant observation in this respect, for though it is often referred to as a method, it is in fact more accurately described as a *role*. The participant or non-participant observer has access to a number of different methods and techniques which can be flexibly used. You can observe, interview, converse, search documents, collect measures or simply 'hang out'. You can use your research role as an instrument; for example, if in observing a school staff meeting you feel uncomfortable or embarrassed, this in itself may tell you something about the nature of the meeting and what is happening in it. What you feel may relate to how the school feels about your being there, or it may be that your feelings echo what others feel. Either way your feelings, rather than being simply 'noise' in the system, give you a starting point for possible further investigation. Similarly, if, as a woman, you feel ignored, not taken seriously or dismissed by senior staff in the school, this too may tell you something about the character of the school that you can use as a starting point for research. Reinterpreting what may be felt as a personal response into social terms is a process often not acknowledged as a research technique, but it is one that is valuable to learn both for the benefit of research and for self-preservation! The point is that in the reactions you create in a field role, the field reveals something of itself to you; what you have to learn is how to use this information productively. A classic example is given by Barry MacDonald from one of his interviews conducted as part of the Humanities Curriculum Project evaluation:

TEACHER: Don't expect me to tell you anything about the Head.
MACDONALD: You just have.

You might find the suggestion that you use subjectivity in this way in itself unscientific, but there is no reason for not using subjective impressions as starting points for trying to get more conventionally objective data. The point is to select significant questions to pursue, a process which is inevitably one involving judgement, and so equally inevitably a subjective element.

The research project, too, can become its own instrument in a participative study. I described earlier how, in studying the work of school inspectors, I used a process of regular reporting-back to the inspectors in order both to sustain their interest and support for the research and to establish a degree of collaboration in the study. Again there are those who will say that to do this is unscientific since it contaminates the data and may bias the interpretation, so threatening objectivity. There are research problems, and ways of conceiving research, where this is undoubtedly the case; but applied research in education may demand a different conception overall, for in education the distance between those who are the subjects of research and those who execute it is remarkably small. Educational research is, in itself, an educational activity and an educational process. It will often include its subjects in its audience, and so it would seem sensible to design projects and carry them out with learning in mind. This is not to advocate a heavy instructional hand, for to use research as a means of propaganda would be inappropriate, counter-productive and non-educational.

This is an important point which has implications for the selection of problems, issues and topics for research, for if learning is to be built into the research process, it follows that tasks should be chosen where there is considerable, and perhaps continuing, uncertainty on the part of those involved, including the researcher. This too may seem to fly in the face of convention, which tends to see researchers as experts, and research as an activity exclusively carried out by those at the pinnacle of achievement in a field of knowledge. I am suggesting that, on the contrary, research should be carried out by people who do not know the answers to the problems they are investigating, that they should see their learning as involving their subjects in learning too, and that they should avoid foreclosing on recommendations whenever possible. But to state this view at this point is perhaps to run ahead of the text. I mention it here because I want to point to another appealing aspect of participant observation, which is its capacity as a means of learning.

One of the reasons for the widespread use of participant observation in recent years has been because it appears to offer a means of relating research to those in relatively low-status roles in the education system – particularly to teachers, and in a few cases to pupils. (Willis (1977), for example, offers us an appendix in which his book is reviewed by the 'Lads' who are its subject.) Measurement research of the kind conventionally used by educational research in the recent past, relying heavily on testing or survey methods, is invariably directed upwards within education systems. Its designed intention is to affect policy and policy decisions. Thus the work of sociologists of education in the 1950s and 1960s was often specifically intended as an attack on 11+ selection, an attack formulated in terms of the rhetoric which the system used to defend itself. This research attempted to show that selection, intended to give working-class children access to grammar schools, in fact typically selected in terms of criteria that were primarily of a social class nature.

Such research was, and is, important and I do not want to minimize its significance. It is, however, research that is directed at those, mainly outside schools, who take decisions about what goes on inside. It was this research that created the basis, or at least the language, that in Britain made possible the establishment of a comprehensive secondary school system. It was research that in one sense raised no questions at all about the structure of the decision-taking system, but directed all its efforts to influencing one decision. In that sense it was both successful and limited to one kind of problem, albeit an enduring and important one.

Research that is directed in this way has more or less consciously to adopt a language, a style, and to find friends that lend it credibility. It has to develop a style that is convincing, credible and usable to those who constitute its audience. Carefully selected and well-packaged statistics are a prime case, and indeed in the eyes of many are synonymous with 'research'.

Such statistics fit well the dialogues of politicians, administrators, managers and the press. They are less comfortable as part of the natural language of teachers or indeed of anyone else once the spotlight of public attention is turned away.

If the research problem is one that addresses relatively routine aspects of school and classroom practice, and sees teachers, pupils and perhaps parents as being the subjects and the primary audience for the study, then the use of other research forms becomes appropriate. The task, then, is to find forms of reporting and styles of presentation that easily enter the natural language, dialogue and styles of thought of those concerned. The sharp and selective use of statistics will often be inappropriate, as will the clipped and concise civil service style of report, or the heavy language of interpretive sociology. So, too, may be long, unedited transcripts or literally transcribed interviews presented without a helping text. The problem is a difficult and enduring one, and not easily solved. A participant observation role does however offer more of a basis for establishing dialogue between researchers and teachers, pupils and parents, and of providing some basis for making judgements about appropriate styles and forms of reporting, if only because these problems will have reoccurred throughout the research and will be familiar to the researcher. This is why I claim that the decision to adopt a participant observer role may in part be a political decision, for it relates to a decision to report sideways and downwards rather than upwards. Barry MacDonald, in his often quoted typology of evaluation models, terms this a 'democratic' model, to be contrasted with 'autocratic' and 'bureaucratic' models.

Bureaucratic evaluation

Bureaucratic evaluation is an unconditional service to those government agencies which have major control over the allocation of educational resources. The evaluator accepts the values of those who hold office, and offers information which will help them to accomplish their policy objectives. He acts as a management consultant, and his criterion of success is client satisfaction. His techniques of study must be credible to the policy-makers and not lay them open to public criticism. He has no independence, no control over the use that is made of his information, and no court of appeal.

The report is owned by the bureaucracy and lodged in its files. The key concepts of bureaucratic evaluation are 'service', 'utility' and 'efficiency'. Its key justificatory concept is 'the reality of power'.

Autocratic evaluation

Autocratic evaluation is a conditional service to those government agencies which have major control over the allocation of educational resources. It offers external validation of policy in exchange for compliance with its recommendations. Its values are derived from the evaluator's perception of the constitutional and moral obligations of the bureaucracy. He focuses upon issues of educational merit, and acts as expert adviser. His technique of study must yield scientific proofs, because his power base is the academic research community. His contractual arrangements guarantee non-interference by the client, and he retains ownership of the study. His report is lodged in the files of the bureaucracy, but is also published in academic journals. If his recommendations are rejected, policy is not validated. His court of appeal is the research community, and higher levels in the bureaucracy. The key concepts of the autocratic evaluator are 'principle' and 'objectivity'. Its key justificatory concept is 'the responsibility of office'.

Democratic evaluation

Democratic evaluation is an information service to the whole community about the characteristics of an educational programme. Sponsorship of the evaluation study does not in itself confer a special claim upon this service. The democratic evaluator recognises value pluralism and seeks to represent a range of interests in his issue formulation. The basic value is an informed citizenry, and the evaluator acts as a broker in exchanges of information between groups who want knowledge of each other. His techniques of data gathering and presentation must be accessible to non-specialist audiences. His main activity is the collection of definitions of, and reactions to, the programme. He offers confidentiality to informants and gives them control over his use of the information they provide. The report is non-recommendatory, and the evaluator has no concept of inform-ation misuse. The evaluator engages in periodic negotiation of his relationships with sponsors and programme participants. The criterion of success is the range of audiences served. The report aspires to 'best-seller' status. The key concepts of democratic evaluation are 'confidentiality', 'negotiation', and 'accessibility'. The key justifi-catory concept is 'the right to know'.

(MacDonald and Walker, 1974, 17–18)

Behind the somewhat provocative terms used here lies a concern with the inadequacy of an established pattern of research which reports upwards on those occupying relatively low status and having little power. This has become a major issue for social science research as well as for education. 'Whose side are we on?' asks Howard Becker in a strongly partisan statement, to be sharply attacked by Alvin Gouldner for advocating 'underdog sociology' (see Douglas, 1972, for reprints of both statements).

Conclusion

In most standard textbooks you will find discussions about the relative strengths and weaknesses of qualitative as against quantitative methods of research. Qualitative methods, it is said, are subjective, unreliable, unsystematic, lack adequate checks on their validity and are generally speaking unscientific. Quantitative methods, it is counter-argued, are technically inadequate in the face of real problems, usually inappropriately used and fail to explain most of the variance they do reveal. The argument is a pervasive one and in recent years both Cyril Burt and Margaret Mead have been accused by contemporary researchers, who have discovered that they both often failed to apply the methods they so strenuously advocated, and perhaps that they lied in reporting their results. The point that is less often made, and which I have emphasized here, is primarily concerned with different ways of conceiving the relationship between the researcher, the subject and the audience. I have asked, in terms of the political relationship between these different interest groups, whether the intention of the research is genuinely to learn and to encourage learning, or whether it is to propagate a particular view. The further question this raises, which will be taken up later, is whether it is feasible, or indeed wise, to advocate democratic research relationships within organizations that are essentially bureaucratic and hierarchical.

In his paper, 'What counts as research?' (Stenhouse, 1980), Lawrence Stenhouse dismissed the criticism of teacher research that sees teachers as too involved in professional action to be able to conduct objective research, adding, 'In my experience the dedication of professional researchers to their theories is a more serious source of bias than the dedication of teachers to their practice.' This chapter has been predicated on Stenhouse's assumption, but it is important to bear in mind that it is written by someone trained as a professional researcher.

Some time ago, at the conclusion of a long meeting with the head of a primary school to which I was trying to gain access to carry out a research study, the head said to me as I was leaving: 'You know, until I talked to you I thought you must be a sociologist.' The scarcely controlled contempt he brought to the final word does not translate into print. 'I thought you must be a *sociologist*.' The impact of the point did not really strike home until I realized that I had heard the same tone before. I had used it; but I had used it to refer to *headteachers*.

4 Techniques for research

In this chapter I shall look more closely at a range of techniques that might be used in educational research. These techniques will not be described fully as accounts are available in other places; the intention here is to add to conventional descriptions those characteristics of each technique that are relevant to problems of doing educational research in the context of application and practice.

I have chosen to present this chapter in terms of three headings. The first section I have labelled 'Interviews', and have used it to include techniques which are not strictly speaking interviews, but which share generic characteristics with the interview, like questionnaires. Second, I shall look at observational techniques, including the use of video and photography which may be considered extensions of human observation methods. Third, in a section I have called 'Intraviews', I will consider the use of documentary sources that speak from within the institution or from the viewpoint of the people who are the subjects of study – looking at diaries, log books, narratives and timetables.

Interviews

In essence the interview relies on the fact that people are able to offer accounts of their behaviour, practice and actions to those who ask them questions. The interview is, in this sense, a method or a group of techniques specific to the social and human sciences. It includes a wide range of techniques, from the structured questionnaire through to the 'unstructured' conversation, but all hinge on the assumption that people are, to some degree, reflective about their own actions, or can be put in a position where they become so. Implied in the notion of interviewing is a notion of the subject as a researcher, that is as someone able to offer reflective accounts and to test these against experience.

This feature of the interview has brought it to prominence amongst advocates of the teachers-as-researchers 'movement', for it places a degree of authority on the subject and to some extent at least takes for granted that the account that is given has truth value.

QUESTIONNAIRES

The questionnaire may be considered as a formalized and stylized interview, or interview by proxy. The form is the same as it would be in a face-to-face interview, but in order to remove the interviewer the subject is presented with what, essentially, is a structured transcript with the responses missing. The questionnaire is like interviewing-by-numbers, and like painting-by-numbers it suffers some of the same problems of mass production and lack of interpretative opportunity. On the other hand it offers considerable advantages in administration – it presents an even stimulus, potentially to large numbers of people simultaneously, and provides the investigator with an easy (relatively easy) accumulation of data.

Questionnaires are often thought of as mainly applicable to large samples and as demanding rather superficial levels of questioning, or least questions that are carefully honed to give preordinately determined answers. They may also be used in more localized and intimate settings. A group of teachers in the Ford Teaching Project (mentioned in Chapter 3) used questionnaires to investigate the conditions of learning among 9- to 12-year-old pupils (Browning *et al.*, n.d.). Their first questionnaire was eminently simple and straightforward:

Questionnaire 1

Name...

Date...

Please try to give an answer to all the questions. Underline the answer you think applies.

1. Did you learn anything new?
   nothing/a little/some/a fair amount/a lot

2. Did you find the session interesting?
   interesting/acceptable/boring

   Can you give a reason? ....

3. Did you understand what you were supposed to do?
   fully/sufficiently/vaguely/not at all

4. Did the teacher talk?   *too much/enough/too little*

5. Did you need any help from the teacher?
   none/a little/some/a fair amount/a lot

6. Were you able to get the help you needed from the teacher?
   straight away/after a little while/after some time/after a long time
   If you had to wait for help, or never got help, can you give a reason? ....

7. Did you ask for help from outside your group?
   frequently/occasionally/not at all

8. Could you find all the things you needed?
   all of them/most of them/some of them/a few of them/none of them

9. Were you interrupted by other people outside your group?
   frequently/occasionally/not at all

10. If you were delayed was it caused by?
    going out/unable to talk to teacher/someone coming into the room/unable to concentrate/lack of equipment/any other reason

---

Here is a space for you to write any other comments about the session. You may continue on the other side if you wish.

Analysis sheet for first questionnaire

1. Did you learn anything new?

nothing	a little	some	a fair amount	a lot

2. Did you find the session interesting?

interesting	acceptable	boring

3. Did you understand what you were supposed to do?

fully	sufficiently	vaguely	not at all

4. Did the teacher talk?

too much	enough	too little

5. Did you need any help from teacher?

none	a little	a fair amount	a lot

6. Were you able to get the help you needed from the teacher?

straight away	after a little while	after some time	after a long time

7. Did you ask for help from outside your group?

frequently	occasionally	not at all

8. Could you find all the things you needed?

all of them	most of them	some of them	a few of them	none of them

9. Were you interrupted by other people outside your group?

frequently	occasionally	not at all

10. If you were delayed was it caused by?

going out	unable to talk to teacher	someone coming into the room	unable to concentrate	lack of equipment	any other reason

(Browning *et al.*, n.d., 6, 7)

A later version of the questionnaire, which took into account experience with this first version, and the responses of the children in terms of what they felt they wanted to be able to say, was considerably more complex and detailed, as shown below. Interestingly this development is the reverse of that normally associated with the development of large-scale questionnaires, which as they are tested tend to become shorter and simpler as ambiguity and open questions are monitored and removed.

Questionnaire 2

Name ....   Subject ....
Date ....
Please answer all the questions by marking in the appropriate 'box'.

1. Did you learn anything new?

nothing	a little	some	a fair amount	a lot

Was this because you were recording (writing up, etc.) your discoveries?

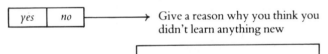

yes	no

→ Give a reason why you think you didn't learn anything new

2. Did you find the session:

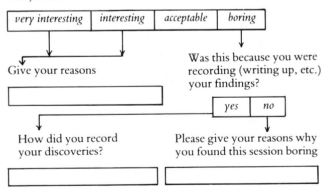

very interesting	interesting	acceptable	boring

Give your reasons

Was this because you were recording (writing up, etc.) your findings?

yes	no

How did you record your discoveries?

Please give your reasons why you found this session boring

3. Did you notice any difference about the session?

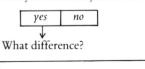

yes	no

What difference?

4. Were you working from any of the following? If not go on to Question 5.

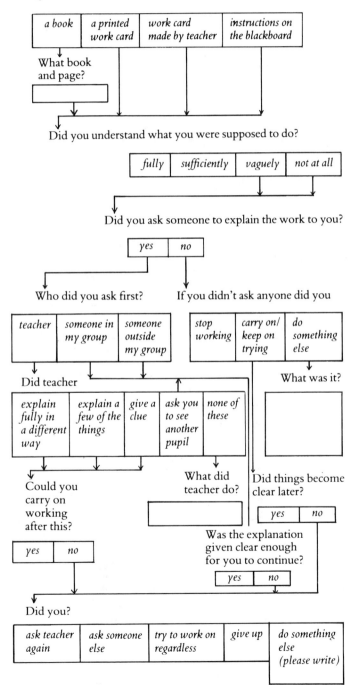

| a book | a printed work card | work card made by teacher | instructions on the blackboard |

What book and page?

Did you understand what you were supposed to do?

| fully | sufficiently | vaguely | not at all |

Did you ask someone to explain the work to you?

| yes | no |

Who did you ask first?   If you didn't ask anyone did you

| teacher | someone in my group | someone outside my group | | stop working | carry on/ keep on trying | do something else |

Did teacher   What was it?

| explain fully in a different way | explain a few of the things | give a clue | ask you to see another pupil | none of these |

Could you carry on working after this?   What did teacher do?   Did things become clear later?

| yes | no |

Was the explanation given clear enough for you to continue?

| yes | no |

Did you?

| ask teacher again | ask someone else | try to work on regardless | give up | do something else (please write) |

If you did not answer Question 4 you should answer Question 5.

5. How were you working?

from teacher's verbal instructions (talk)	from teacher's suggestions	teacher discusses with you/ group then you choose	from your own ideas	from your group's ideas	something else(please write)

How clear were you as to what you were trying to do?

very clear	some idea	vague idea	only a little idea	no idea

Would you rather have had some written instructions?

yes	no

Is this because you like to have something definite (or clear cut) to work on?

→ What reason?

yes	no

6. Could you find all the things you needed?

all of them	most of them	some of them	a few of them	none of them

Make a list of the things you could not find easily

Was the thing most difficult to find because

you didn't know where it was kept	it is not normally in the class	you looked where it should be but it was missing	it was equipment teacher keeps	someone was using it	of some other reason

Did you find it eventually?

What reason?

yes	no

→ What did you do?

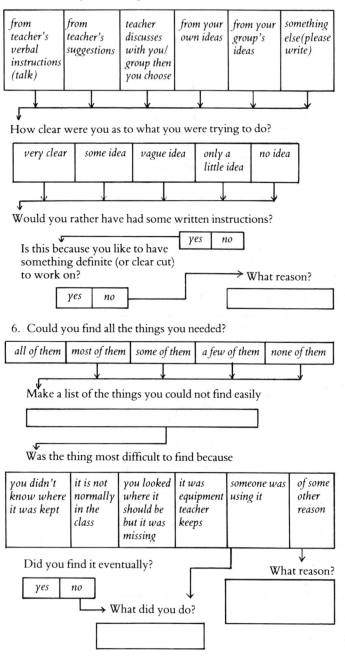

7. Try to estimate how many times you asked for help outside your group. Put a circle around your estimate.

0 1 2 3 4 5 6 7 8 9 10 more than 10

Try to recall your most difficult problem and then answer the following. What was your most difficult problem?

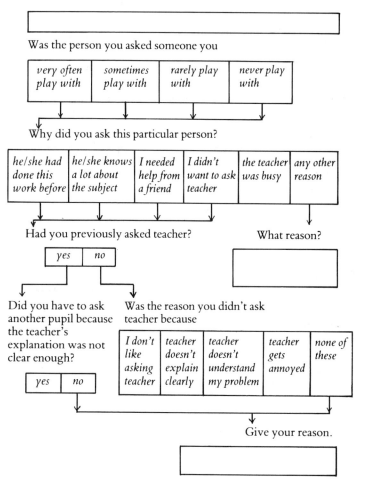

Was the person you asked someone you

very often play with	sometimes play with	rarely play with	never play with

Why did you ask this particular person?

he/she had done this work before	he/she knows a lot about the subject	I needed help from a friend	I didn't want to ask teacher	the teacher was busy	any other reason

Had you previously asked teacher?   What reason?

yes	no

Did you have to ask another pupil because the teacher's explanation was not clear enough?

Was the reason you didn't ask teacher because

I don't like asking teacher	teacher doesn't explain clearly	teacher doesn't understand my problem	teacher gets annoyed	none of these

yes	no

Give your reason.

8. Did you have sufficient time to do the work you wanted, or had, to do?

too much time	plenty of time	enough time	just enough time	needed more time	far too little time

9. Try to estimate how many times you were interrupted from outside your group. Put a circle round your estimate.

0 1 2 3 4 5 6 7 8 9 10 more than 10

If you were interrupted from outside your group think about the longest delay caused to your work and then answer the following questions.

Was the person who interrupted someone you

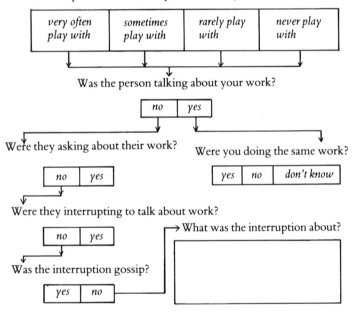

very often play with	sometimes play with	rarely play with	never play with

Was the person talking about your work?

no	yes

Were they asking about their work?   Were you doing the same work?

no	yes

yes	no	don't know

Were they interrupting to talk about work?

no	yes

→ What was the interruption about?

Was the interruption gossip?

yes	no

10. Were you working in a group this session?

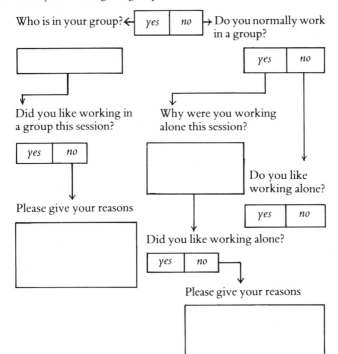

Who is in your group? ← | yes | no | → Do you normally work in a group?

| yes | no |

Did you like working in a group this session?

| yes | no |

Please give your reasons

Why were you working alone this session?

Do you like working alone?

| yes | no |

Did you like working alone?

| yes | no |

Please give your reasons

11. How well were you able to concentrate throughout the session?

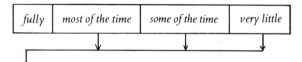

fully	most of the time	some of the time	very little

Was your concentration spoilt by any of the following?
You may indicate in more than one 'box' if you wish.

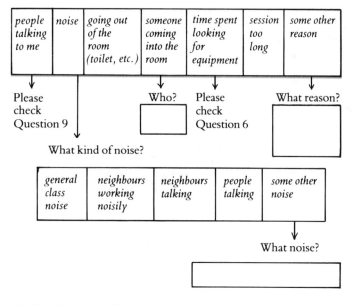

people talking to me	noise	going out of the room (toilet, etc.)	someone coming into the room	time spent looking for equipment	session too long	some other reason

Please check Question 9

What kind of noise?

Who?

Please check Question 6

What reason?

general class noise	neighbours working noisily	neighbours talking	people talking	some other noise

What noise?

12. Here is a space where you may write any other comments about the session or the work you were doing.

Section from Analysis Chart A for Questionnaire 2

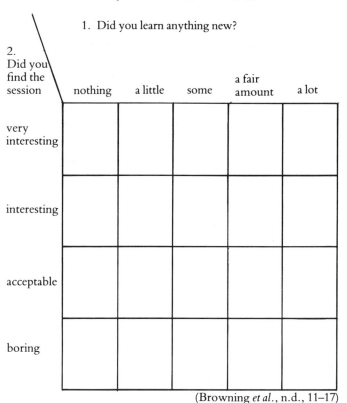

(Browning *et al.*, n.d., 11–17)

When questionnaires are used in small-scale intimate settings they can be used with a sense of risk that would not be possible when they are used for collecting responses from large samples through direct mailing or by making use of trained inter-viewers. This is possible because in face-to-face contact there are opportunities for cross-checking, fast turn-around of information and generally a higher redundancy in communi-cation than is present when the researcher faces large quantities of anonymous returns. This is perhaps why many of the standard texts on questionnaire design, while they offer much advice that is appropriate, are sometimes pitched at a level of precision that is inappropriate for the designer of a small-scale study.

In a small-scale study it may be appropriate to break the rules of questionnaire design, for instance by asking taboo questions and by making considerable use of open-ended questions. As an example, Barry MacDonald and I once organized a weekend conference which was designed to collect what we called 'professional life histories' of a group of twenty teachers who had been involved, one way or another, in curriculum innovations:

When we sat down and asked ourselves what we'd like to know about you, these were some of the questions we asked.

Is your background working class or middle class?

....

In politics do you lean to the left/centre/right?

....

Do you have any strong religious beliefs?

....

How do you feel about the Raising of the School Leaving Age?

....

If you had the power to change one thing in the education system, what change would you bring about?

....

Do you see yourself as a career teacher?

....

Is promotion important to you?

....

If you weren't in teaching how would you prefer to earn a living?

....

Do you think teachers are, or could be, an important influence on the lives of the children they teach?

....

The intention here is very different from the intention that lies behind a multiple-choice questionnaire designed for large-scale mail distribution. The questions are 'real questions' in that we could only guess the kind of answers we might receive and did not know quite what to expect. The intention was not simply to ask questions in order to secure answers for later analysis but rather to set signposts, to indicate a tone, to set going a line of thought and analysis. Given that we were to spend a weekend with the respondents pursuing questions of motivation in relation to curriculum innovation, we wanted from the start to indicate that we were interested in certain kinds of data. In this sense the questions were as important as the answers.

Once the size of the sample expands and communicative redundancy becomes reduced, so questionnaires have to become more precise and carefully tested. It is however still possible to retain some of the open-ended quality of the small-scale questionnaire, if this is desired, by linking it to other information. For example, in a study of science curricula in eleven school districts in the USA, Stake and Easley (1977) designed questionnaires which were mailed out to a sample of a thousand or so people and which managed to incorporate case-study material. They assembled 'scenarios' from drafts of the case studies, tested these in site-visit interviews, and then wrote them into questionnaires, as in the following example:

Scenario Y: Personal bias in teaching

The National Science Foundation has been explicit in including social studies or sciences along with mathematics and science in its definition of science education. This definition provided the opportunity to investigate two issues that are of special interest in the social sciences. First, it was desirable to investigate how the scientific method of inquiry is perceived as applied to social studies and the prevalence of its use. Second, perhaps more than the other two disciplines, social studies include topics of potential controversy and possibly are more prone to contamination by personal bias.

A conversation between the teacher and students in an American history classroom is the setting for this scenario. Four groups were asked to respond to the scenario: social studies teachers in grades 7 through 9, social studies teachers in grades 10 through 12, high school seniors and parents of high school seniors.

Extract from the questionnaire

Please consider the following situation:

At Metro High School, Mr Robinson's American History class is studying immigration and the settlement of America, noting particularly how immigrants have influenced the growth of their city. Here is dialogue midway through Monday's class:

MR ROBINSON: After the Irish immigration of the 1840s and after the importation of Chinese laborers, what other waves of immigration occurred? Sally?

SALLY: Europeans around 1890 and then again after World War I.

MR ROBINSON: Good, I guess that's when we got our Polish jokes. right? (no one laughs) Well, let's see. What sort of long-time trend are we studying?

SHERMAN: People coming to America.

MR ROBINSON: Why did they come, Tammie?

TAMMIE: To come to a country with freedom.

DOUG: (sarcastically) Like freedom to pick cotton.

MR ROBINSON: Well, let's think about that. Some of the early colonists *were* seeking freedom. Were the Chinese who came after the Civil War seeking freedom? (no answer) What were they looking for? (no answer) What were the Irish looking for?

WENDY: Food!

MR ROBINSON: Food more than freedom? Let's make a list of possible reasons for immigrating, then consider each one.

ERIC: My dad says we should be studying how to send them back where they came from rather than how they got here.

MR ROBINSON: Okay, that's an idea. After we make our list of reasons for immigration, let's figure out who wanted the immigrants here and who didn't want them. And then let's decide whether I should be sent back to Africa or Europe.

Mr Robinson is asking questions about history and joking about it. What is your reaction to his teaching style?

— It is fine for some teachers to teach this way. It gets their attention
— I find it offensive
— I don't mind, but he is not likely to get the job done
— Other (fine in principle but not in this case)
— Other (please indicate)

Do teachers and students talk like this in your school(s)?
— Yes, lots do
— Yes, a few do
— No
— Other

Mr Robinson seems reluctant to accept the idea that most immigrants came to America seeking freedom. Let us suppose that this is a bias of his. How important is it for social studies teachers to keep their biases to themselves?
— They should recognize their biases and keep them to themselves
— They should speak honestly as to how they feel on matters
— They should tell how they feel, but present alternative views too
— Other

Suppose Mr Robinson was leading up to a critical analysis of the free enterprise system. Suppose he intended to say that the system was dishonest, that it was cruel in the way it imported cheap labor from foreign lands to work in this country. Do you feel that it would be inappropriate for Mr Robinson to acquaint the students with his conclusions about the free enterprise system in early America?

— It would be right, in fact it is his responsibility to be frank
— It would be all right as long as he indicated his value-orientation
— It is ethically proper, but he would be foolish to do so
— It is wrong for him to use his position for teaching those things
— Other (please explain)

Some parents believe that certain topics should be left out of science and social studies courses, topics such as evolution of the species, human reproduction, and family attitudes and customs. Some parents want such things taught, and of course, want them taught well. – We need to find out how you feel about *using federal funds* for development of teaching materials that include such controversial topics.

— Federal funds should never be spent on such development
— It is all right to spend federal funds this way if it will not cause trouble
— It is important to provide federal support for such development
— Other

In what ways have budget cuts in your district *seriously* affected the social studies curriculum? (Check one or more)

— We have not had budget cuts recently
— The social studies curriculum has not been seriously affected in any way
— Classes have been larger in size
— Needed and highly qualified teachers have been 'let go' and not replaced
— We have more teaching from textbooks, less with materials or in the field
— No longer can we provide a textbook for each student individually
— The inservice training program has been cut back substantially
— Other (please indicate)

As you look at social studies courses in your high school and elsewhere, you probably see things that concern you. Please check those things that you consider to be major problems. (Check as many as you wish)

— Too much emphasis on facts, not enough on concepts
— Too much emphasis on concepts, not enough on facts

— Too much emphasis on teaching about personal values
— Not enough emphasis on teaching about personal values
— Not enough qualified teachers
— Belief that teachers teaching the same course should teach the same things

(Stake and Easley, 1977, 75–80)

This approach to questionnaire design promises to provide a form of integration between 'qualitative' and 'quantitative' forms of data, though you should be warned that Stake and Easley's experience was that such integration was harder to achieve than they thought. First, it proved difficult to extract scenarios from case study data: they almost always had to be rewritten in order to make them usable questionnaire items. Second, in analysing the resulting data the responses to the questionnaires did not easily fit with the case study material, or at least did not provide the kind of straightforward corroboration or refutation of the case studies that might have been expected.

In relation to case studies questionnaires can be used to provide a stimulus to the reader. For example, I followed a descriptive case study of the work of a team of school advisers (inspectors) with a questionnaire, written for those who were the subjects of the study, in order to go beyond the descriptive account and begin the interpretative process. This questionnaire was therefore designed to be speculative and analytic, to go beyond the data I had available, and to draw those who were the subjects of the study into the work of interpreting it.

The observational work of LEA inspectors and advisers

Questions to the advisory team on the basis of the descriptive and narrative accounts (extracts).

3   The adviser in the classroom

3.1 Advisers have to guess at what is hidden from them more than they can observe directly. Each glimpse of a classroom becomes shorthand for a set of extrapolations derived from experience.
Comment

Test: When were you last surprised by something you saw happen in a classroom?

3.2 Eve and Colin both put a major stress on their presentation-of-self in managing their relationships with schools, through dress, appearance, editing of what they say and their behaviour.
Is this typical adviser behaviour?
Example

What considerations do you take into account when:
a) visiting a prestigious secondary school
b) attending an interview for a secondary headship
c) running an in-service course at the Teachers Centre
d) visiting the University
e) attending an Afro-Caribbean evening at a Primary School.

6   The nature of the system

6.1 I have taken the view that the system is characterised by being simultaneously hierarchal and loosely connected. That is to say that each adviser enjoys a high degree of autonomy but suffers a degree of isolation (and fears of being ineffectual). The adviser has little power but a good deal of influence.
Comment

6.2 The main currency in which advisers deal is information. What is significant is not what they know but how much and when. The information they have access to is largely trivial, but they have it before anyone else and that creates the base for their political power within the system.
Comment

Test: Is gossip important to you?

6.8 A formal assertion.
The culture of the system is one in which individual autonomy survives within an overall hierarchy. The cost for the advisers is a degree of isolation (as felt from within), and of inefficiency and ineffectiveness (as perceived from without). The causes are deeper than the management system level and relatively unaffected by changes in the management structure. Attempts to exert greater control over advisers, and to create more efficient management

structures have only a limited effect before the high entropy level inherent in the system reasserts itself.
Comment

This questionnaire was intended to go beyond what I knew. It was not designed to obtain answers to questions I had derived from theoretical speculation but was part of an attempt to test out my own interpretations derived from observation and interviews. In this sense it was the precursor to a first draft of the report. Writing to a select audience of knowledgeable people allowed me to break many of the rules and conventions of questionnaire design.

THE FACE-TO-FACE INTERVIEW

This might seem a strange term to use, but I have been describing ways of using questionnaires that are primarily qualitative, and which take the form of written conversations; a form of structured correspondence if you like. In order to distinguish this from conversational interviews I have adopted the term 'face-to-face interview', though in doing so I immediately have to qualify it, for there are those who would claim that posture, seating position and the angle at which interviewee and interviewer face each other is crucial. Lawrence Stenhouse, for example, has advocated sitting side-by-side rather than face-to-face as if to symbolize the fact that interviewee and interviewer together face a common task, rather than confront one another. Others find this creates communication difficulties and that people facing one another talk more freely and fluently, given the support of non-verbal signals. One exception I have found is the interview conducted during car journeys; as hitch-hikers know, driver-passenger conversations may become interviews of a particularly informative kind. A side-by-side interview to be avoided is to accept invitations with prospective interviewees to talk while jogging, unless you are skilled at running backwards.

Just as questionnaires may be more or less highly structured, so interviews may be more or less planned in advance. Here, as in discussing questionnaires, I have tended to concentrate on unstructured interviews because these tend to be poorly accounted for in standard texts, while structured interviews are fairly thoroughly described elsewhere.

An early decision that faces most interviewers is how to record. It is tempting to use tape recording in order to obtain the fullest and most accurate record; on the other hand many people find tape recording intrusive and cumbersome. Barry MacDonald and Jack Sanger have given an exhaustive account of the advantages and disadvantages of recording as opposed to note taking (MacDonald and Sanger, 1982). I have included here their summary table, which considers the characteristics, strengths and weaknesses of each technique under the headings of generation, processing and reporting of data.

These tables provide a closely written summary of each technique. What is particularly interesting is that the comparison reveals that tape recording and note taking emerge not simply as alternative techniques for achieving similar ends, but as really quite different ways of going about doing research. I suggested that Stake and Easley found something similar when they attempted to marry questionnaire techniques with descriptive case study, and tape recording and note taking, too, turn out to be more different than they at first seem. They each imply a different kind of relationship between the researcher and the task and between the researcher and the subject, and a different conception of the nature of the task. Thus parallel studies carried out using the two different approaches would be likely to be less similar than might be predicted in advance. Note taking draws the researcher into interpretation early in the study and in one sense makes the researcher more of a person in the eyes of the subject. Tape recording lends itself to a recessive style on the part of the researcher, disguising the interpretive process by burying it in the editing and selection of extracts from transcripts. Of course at later stages in the study these positions can be altered and reversed, but initially each technique provides this initial impetus or inclination. Selection is partly a matter of personal preference, partly a question of fitting the technique to the task or to the nature of the setting.

Behind much of this discussion is a view of the interview as an arena for negotiation between the researcher and the subject.

Table 1 Tape recording

	Characteristics	Strengths	Weaknesses
Data generation			
Effectiveness	Personalized relationship. Conversational style. Continuous discourse. Sustained multisensory communication. Interviewer as listener	Naturalistic. Prolific. Penetrative of experience. Tolerant of ambiguity, anecdotalism, inconclusiveness.	Selective but mindless record. Data overload. Favors the articulate. Machine-phobia. Visible data lost.
Fairness	Confidential but on-the-record. Interviewee control emphasized, but hazards unknown, and minimal indication of the value or likely use of the data.	Testimony as 'draft'. Authority vested in objective record. Emphasis on generation maximizes opportunity to testify.	High-risk testimony encouraged. Consequences of disclosure difficult to estimate. Overreliant on interviewer integrity and interviewee judgment.
Validity	Insulated from consequences. Structured by the truth holder. Told to a person.	Raw data preserved in verifiable form. Stimulus as well as response recorded. Time to search for truths. Freedom to tell. Safe responses quickly exhausted and superseded. Dissimulation hard to sustain under continuous observation	Off-the-cuff data. Freedom to lie. Pressure on interviewee to be 'interesting'. Machine-phobia. Overreliant on interviewee self-knowledge.

	Characteristics	Strengths	Weaknesses
Data processing			
Effectiveness	Record transcribed. Transcript sent to interviewee for improvement and release. Interviewee invited to: (a) amend or delete, (b) extend, develop, (c) prioritize, indicate high-risk data. Uncontentious data may be summarized. Deadline for return stipulated.	Data retains much of its original form. Considered testimony. Inaccuracies corrected. Additional data obtained. More clues to interviewee's values and valuables, a guide to negotiable reporting. Interviewee's responsibility for the product is explicit.	Costly. Time consuming. Obsolescent. Loss of valuable data. Inadequacy of verbal record.
Fairness	Negotiation confidential. Interviewee the arbiter. Access to record. Governed by agreed rules, but 'release' can be seen as a 'chicken run' test for the foolhardy.	Interviewee rights respected. Time and opportunity given to change testimony, to calculate risks and benefits. Interviewee free to consult others, to take advice. Possession of transcript and agreement constitute insurance against abuse.	Interviewee asked to release not knowing: (a) how the data will be reported, or (b) norms of disclosure. Interviewee may be poor judge of own interests. Transcripts lower self-esteem.
Validity	Characterized by set sequence of moves open to scrutiny. Based on objective record.	Depends on the argument that given the power and the responsibility for making known their own truths, interviewees will make more effort to do so.	No data on the context of response. Relies overmuch on the interviewee's belief in and commitment to the evaluation mission.

Table 1—continued

	Characteristics	Strengths	Weaknesses
Data reporting			
Effectiveness	Aspires to theatrical form of oral history. Interviews provide subscripts in program drama, interwoven in chronological, scene-by-scene construction. Draft showing data in context negotiated simultaneously with interviewees. Draft rewritten in response to respondent critiques. Final report public.	Naturalistic autobiographical data has inherent dramatic form. Rashomon effect—multiple perspectives. Dramatic imperative overrides interviewee's discretionary impulse. Surrogate experience for the reader. Yields better understandings of what has happened, challenges social beliefs underlying program policy and action.	Slow delivery. Lacking in scientific respectability. Inconclusiveness. Overlengthy due to irreducible obligations to individuals. Costly to produce and disseminate.
Fairness	Draft report confidential to interviewee group. Rewritten to satisfy interviewee criticism. But in negotiation the evaluator presses: (a) audience concerns and needs, (b) dramatic values.	Interviewee participation. Form of the report foreshadowed by the form of the interview. Individual testimony highly valued. Natural language maximizes accessibility to nonspecialist readers and to subjects.	Evaluator allocates 'star' and 'support' status. Evaluator alone has all the data. Interviewee cannot retract released data.

Validity	Individual bias, censorship, inaccuracy subject to correction through consultation with knowledgeable and multivariate constituency. Account open to external challenge based on cited testimony or back-up tapes, but – artistic values may intrude.	'Pluralist' endorsement of account as accurate, relevant, balanced. Triangulation of oral histories. Autobiographical emphasis. Appeals to reader's own experience.	Context of generation disappears. Role and influence of evaluator underemphasized. Formal imperatives override substantive. Genre makes the account dismissable as factoid.

Table 2 Note taking

	Characteristics	Strengths	Weaknesses
Data generation			
Effectiveness	Structured roles. Working relationship. Question/Answer style. Episodic discourse. Interviewer as informed questioner and ethnographer of communication.	Only what is 'finished' and valued is recorded, so interviewee's stumbles, confusions, incoherences, irrelevances are weeded out or improved and polished. Professional control of the record. Penetrative of meaning and salience. Parsimonious.	Reductionist. Interviewee deference to recording task constrains natural discourse, invites closure and conservatism and resultant lack of penetration. Reduced nonverbal contact.
Fairness	Private except for what is noted – and remains so. Open notebook offers interviewee cumulative evidence of data value. (Even closed notes indicate selection criteria.) Time out to write and check entries enhances interviewee control of testimony.	Low-risk testimony the norm. Afford the security of the conventional recording medium. Emphasis on role performance rather than role experience protects the person.	No chance to reconsider testimony or its representation. Tendency for interviewer's structures to organize the data. Reliance upon interviewer's skill with shorthand/encoding.
Validity	Emphasis on public outcomes minimizes lazy, careless, or unsupportable testimony. But – no objective record; limited verbatim data.	Nonverbal as well as verbal components of communication taken into account. Interviewer uses knowledge and skills to cross-check, represent other viewpoints, challenge testimony.	Little raw data survives. Most data has been treated at source in some way. Difficult to respect informal, non-propositional forms of knowledge and understanding.

	Characteristics	Strengths	Weaknesses
Data processing			
Effectiveness	Negotiation of noted summary in biographic form for improvement and release. Interviewee invited to: (a) authorize the representation (b) rewrite, and (c) add.	Summaries facilitate faster data negotiation and clearance. Economical in time and cost. Clearance facilitated as summary approximates to recall of event.	Difficult to use data except in individual interview packages. Paucity of raw data. Understandings of data prematurely fixed. No reselection of raw data possible.
Fairness	Absence of high-risk data reduces need for confidentiality. Joint arbitration of processed accounts. Interviewee can totally reject the account as inconsistent with his recall of event.	Nature of summary affords less threatening accounts. Summaries evidence evaluator's style and likely use of data—signals that inform and 'arm' respondent against later abuse. Economical, intelligible forms facilitate interviewee task in negotiating clearance.	Packaged nature of summaries deters from deleting/adding to accounts. Respondent's private interests underrepresented Empathy/sympathy with interviewee at mercy of writer's skill. Lack of independent record may lead (a) strong interviewees to disclaim account; (b) weak interviewees to accept account.
Validity	High premium placed upon interviewer's skill and integrity in selection, analysis, and synthesis of data. Accounts of particular testimony structured in terms of their contribution to generalized validity of program overview.	Rich data on context of response. Interviewer's skill, interests and overall knowledge enable valuation, validation, and rationalization of data.	Interviewer error/bias in generation compounded at advanced processing stage. Lack of objective evidence to substantiate analysis. Vulnerable to facile causal interference Autobiography treated as biography

	Characteristics	Strengths	Weaknesses
Data reporting			
Effectiveness	Biographical portrayal or narrative account of the program experience, with individual cameos. Thematic or issues organization. Interviews treated piecemeal or as epitomes of the program story.	Condensed and susceptible to summary. Complex features noted but integrated. Commonalities emphasized. Parsimonious use of raw data to support or illustrate. Offers a synthesis of understanding.	Individuals submerged in overview or lost in 'group' perspectives. An outsider's account of insiders.
Fairness	Deemphasis on individual testimony. Opportunities to comment, adverse comments noted and reported, usually as addenda.	Individuals protected because their testimonies are subsumed in framework of understanding.	Interviewees dependent on sympathetic evaluator as spokesman for their realities. Importance of individuals as actors diminished. Interviewees deskilled as critics by literary construction and by lack of source data record.
Validity	Emphasis on contextualization, coherence, contingency. Inherent logic forms in summarizing afford critique. Constructs explicit.	Interviewer, with skills, interests and knowledge, is the most qualified to judge authenticity, relatedness, and resulting hierarchies of data importance. Interviewer's commitment is to the 'greater truths'. Interviewer accountable to academic peers.	Loss of individual voices. Final reports are summaries of summaries – high possibility of gross reductionism, compounded error, and heavy skewing. Reliance on interviewer as storyteller increases systematic bias. No objective raw data to support the account.

Interviews can be conceived as data-collection devices which attempt to capture the responses of people to questions that are carefully standardized and intended to be minimally interventive: the image is one of skimming from the subject's consciousness a series of statements, views or attitudes. Anyone who has been interviewed, even on trivial topics (such as which television programmes they watched last week), will know that the interview is a rare enough event for it to leave a mark on the interviewee. You find yourself rethinking what you said, aware of the gaps between what you wanted to say and what you were able to say. When interviewed on deeper topics, such as how you see your work, or relationships within the family, or your feelings about death, the effect is more marked. The interview both opens up areas of dialogue in taken-for-granted areas of your life, and at the same time, perhaps because of the conversational asymmetry in the relationship between the interviewer and the interviewee, fails to offer a sense of closure. As a result the interviewee typically emerges from the interview with a feeling of being left stranded. It is the researcher who goes away with the data to rework it in his or her own fashion, to gain satisfaction from making it make sense, and who indeed has the context to do so.

David Tripp has argued that the interview ought to provide more coherence for the subject. It should (for social science reasons) attempt to understand, take on board and explore what the interviewee's questions are as well as pursuing only the interviewer's agenda:

Thus an attempt to record what someone thinks on a particular question must also include the attempt to discover how that question and its relevant features is placed in the world-view of the interviewee, that is in the interviewee's rather than the interviewer's terms. In this regard it must be equally important to the interviewer to learn what questions are important to the interviewee, as it is to learn the answers to questions considered important by the interviewer. One way of achieving this is to allow the interviewee, at the very least, joint responsibility for structuring the interview in terms of the progress of questions, in content, kind, sequence and number. One is thus dealing with questions of power: the extent to which power is equally shared, or in this case, the symmetry of the communication.

(Tripp, 1983a, 4–5)

For the interviewer alert to the issue it is not difficult to frame the interview in ways that at least provide the opportunity for reflection and processing within the interview itself. For example, pausing at intervals and asking the interviewee to recapitulate and to summarize, or even offering summaries and asking for an assessment of your own understanding; explaining initially what your intention is and asking for critical responses; leaving tapes with the interviewee to allow him or her to listen back to what was said and to comment on it; corresponding with people after an interview. All these things are possible and may be appropriate in some instances. They relate in part, as David Tripp argues, to a more complete understanding, but also at a procedural level to problems of exit. The word in itself comes as a surprise. We are familiar with problems of access, and research texts tend to discuss access problems and how they might be overcome at some length. Less often do we talk about making exits, either at the level of the interview or at the level of the study.

Taking the interview in this direction does of course have serious implications in terms of staffing. Most large-scale projects are unable to think of the interview in such terms because they operate on the assumption that interviewers will be relatively low-status people with specialized interviewing training but without a grasp of the essential research questions. In such terms it is necessary to develop a view of the interview that is predominantly technical: that is to say, a view that sees the interview as a technique in which people can be trained, and which is transferable from one project to another without too much difficulty.

For most student projects it is not feasible or appropriate to hire interviewers. They tend to be small-scale, one-person projects in which the student does pretty well everything, and most of it on his or her own. It makes sense therefore to make full use of the strengths and advantages of the situation, rather than to attempt to mimic techniques that are really only appropriate to large-scale studies. The problem is compounded by the fact that it is the work of large-scale studies that mostly informs textbook writers (including this one!). The difficulty, I think, is in drawing a line between the standards set and the questions raised by professional research and making full use of appropriate techniques.

In these terms education is a special case, for in education those engaging in student-level research may not be contemplating training as professional research workers but intend pursuing their careers within school systems. Educational research is therefore unlike social science research in that a large amount of the research that is done consists of 'student' (i.e. usually teacher) research undertaken in connection with courses of one kind or another.

This creates a number of problems, not least that the 'literature' becomes virtually invisible, or available on a limited basis to only a few people. It puts external examiners in a position that is different from that conventionally defined, for there is little public discourse to which to refer in order to arrive at a sense of standards. To hold student work against the standards of published work is simply inappropriate.

These issues are not unrelated to problems of interviewing. It makes sense for students to use the interview in the way that David Tripp, Charles Hull, Helen Simons, Lawrence Stenhouse and others have suggested. To do so, however, is to cut across many of the conventions implicit in the social science literature, a methodological literature that dominates educational research. It follows that students need to be prepared to argue the case for what they do, and not simply to do it. This in turn demands a high level of self-awareness and reflexivity, not so much at the personal level (though that too may be necessary) but at an academic level. You have to ask yourself: What am I doing? Why? How do I justify it?

With every interview and every question it may be necessary to run a second record through your head which asks you these questions. The difficulty is doing this without losing a grip on the interview itself. Once you seem mechanical, unrelaxed, unsure or manipulative you may lose rapport or, more important, trust.

Observations

In the previous section I have tended to overlook the importance of fitting the technique to the task and instead have leapt to discussion of the techniques *per se*. In part this is a consequence of the position I argued earlier, that techniques may search for problems rather than be rationally selected on the basis of a carefully framed formulation of the task. The same may sometimes be true of observations; that is to say, observation may lead to an awareness of a researchable problem rather than strictly following the formulation of the problem.

It is still the case that once a problem has been identified a good deal of work may go into reformulating it in researchable terms and in specifying the kind of techniques that will be used in order to produce usable and relevant data. Boehm and Weinberg (1977) provide a useful and detailed example of the process in relation to a particular problem requiring an observational approach:

Steps to making classroom observations	*Application example*
I. What is the nature of the problem or the question with which you are confronted? Define the problem and the related behaviors clearly.	I. The first-grade teachers at a school located within a large metropolitan area have established a resource center for their pupils. The purpose of the center is to provide an opportunity for the first graders to engage in a variety of learning activities, focusing on the development of beginning reading skills. Each of the school's three first-grade classes spends approximately 25 minutes of each day in the center. During this time, the children complete one task which they have individually selected from a series of 30 learning activities: copying shapes, matching letters with objects depicting that letter

name, classifying objects into concept categories, listening to an audiotape of a story while looking at pictures of that story, and so on. When a child completes a learning activity and has the project checked by the teacher or aide he or she may choose another task. The teachers want to know if their first-grade pupils are able to select, pursue, and complete these tasks independently of teacher, aide, or other pupil assistance.

Problem: Do individual first graders select, pursue, and complete the learning activities without seeking assistance of the teacher, aide, or other pupils?

II. Why would systematic observations be helpful in dealing with this problem or answering the question?

II. The teachers decide that by using observational procedures they will be able to make systematic recordings of the pupils' behavior during their time in the resource center. The teachers could limit their approach to merely looking at completed pupil activities, but by introducing observation of the patterns of pupil behavior in the center the teachers gather a richer pool of information for drawing their conclusions and more directly answering their question about pupil independence. Furthermore, observations over time will provide teachers with an understanding of differences among children in pursuing and completing activities without the assistance of others.

III. What are the relevant characteristics of the setting in which behavior will be observed?

A: What constraint does the physical setting have on possible behaviors?

III. Characteristics of the setting include space, equipment, and people present.

A: *Constraints of the setting:* Because the average first-grade class at the school consists of 25 children, and since a 'standard' sized classroom has been designated as the resource center, the pupils' behavior is limited in its range of mobility. Yet, because of pupil proximity, the setting itself might encourage verbal exchanges and pupils' 'assisting' one another. Of course the availability of the particular learning materials, as opposed to other possible materials, can restrain the scope of behaviors to be viewed.

B: What is the physical arrangement of the various components of the setting that might need to be considered?

B: *Physical arrangement:* Each of 30 tasks are numbered and placed in various locations such as bookshelves, windowsills, corners of the floor, and on tables. Pupil work areas are provided adjacent to the materials.

C: What people will be present in the setting? What characteristics of the individuals or group being observed need to be considered?

C: *People present:* In addition to the 25 pupils in each first-grade class, a class teacher, an aide, and an observer are present in the setting. The aide has been trained beforehand in the use of the learning materials, but has been encouraged to provide assistance only when requested by pupils. The observer will be one of the other first-grade teachers who has arranged a 25-minute free period to coincide with the resource center period of this class.

IV. Given the particular focus of your observations and given your knowledge of the problem area, what is the universe of behaviors that you intend to consider?

IV. The teachers will consider how the pupils:
— Select an activity. (What task does a pupil choose on any given day? What is the range of tasks that he or she chooses over a period of time?)
— Engage in a task. (Do the pupils work with or without requesting

assistance from teacher, aide, or other pupils?)
— Indicate that a given task is completed.
In addition, it might also be interesting to see if there is a relationship between these observed behaviors and the quality of the pupil's final product.

V. What units of behavior or clearly defined categories of behavior will you focus on? In determining your list of categories for classifying observable behavior, consider whether a previously developed observational schedule might be used.

• Decide whether a sign or category system is more appropriate for your problem:
— Are the categories or signs employed mutually exclusive?
— Is the listing of categories or signs exhaustive of the universe of behaviors you wish to consider?

V. In their search of observational schedules already available for use, the teachers were unable to find a recording system including the categories of behaviors that matched the purpose of their observations.

• Since they were interested only in evidence of independent behavior, they adopted a sign system, that is, they generated the following specific categories of behavior for labeling observations:

1. The child *selects* one of the 30 activities, then picks up the materials and takes them to the designated work area. (However, if the child merely looks at the materials without taking them to the work area, this would not be classified as selecting a task.)

2. The child *requests* assistance from the teacher, aide, or another pupil in the resource center by either gesturing for assistance, verbally asking for assistance, or combining gesture and verbal request. (However, if the child asks to get a drink of water or merely talks to the teacher, aide, or another pupil, this would not be classified as a request for assistance.)

3. The child *indicates* that a given task has been completed by showing the product to the teacher or aide. (However, if the child partially completes the task, he or she would be encouraged to resume work on the task – but this would not constitute a request for assistance.)

VI. What sampling procedure (time or event) will most effectively enable you to record representative observations?

A: Will all the people in the setting be observed, or will you select a representative sample?

VI. The teachers decided which children would be observed and at what frequency.

A: Since it would be impossible for an individual teacher to observe all children simultaneously, it is necessary to observe a sample of children each day and to order the observations of their behavior systematically. Therefore, the teachers adopted a time-sampling procedure, that is they decided to observe a preselected sample of five children each day. Consequently, by the end of a five-day school week each of the 25 children will have been observed during one of the daily sessions in the resource center.

B: How frequently across time should you observe so that your conclusions have adequate observational support?

B: In order to observe each of the five children at different points in the work period, the teacher-observer observes each of the five children to be observed that day at work for one minute during a five-minute segment. The teacher then proceeds to observe each of the five for one minute for the second five-minute segment, and so forth until each of the five children has been observed for a total of four minutes. This procedure is followed each day of the week, five children at a time, until all 25 children have been observed.

C: To what extent does the subject of the observation need to be viewed in a variety of settings and activities within the school in order to deal adequately with

C: Does not apply to this particular observation problem.

the particular problem or
question?

VII. How confident are you
that your observation
schedule facilitates
reliable observations?
How might you verify
this?

VII. To determine the
reliability of the
observational scheme,
two of the three first-
grade teachers might
observe the resource
center period of the third
teacher on two
consecutive days. The
degree to which the two
raters agreed with each
other in recording the
instances of request for
assistance could then be
determined. The percent
of agreement in
indicating the pupil's
selection of tasks could
also be determined by
this procedure. A high
rate of agreement would
indicate a high level of
reliability between the
observers.

VIII. What inferences or
conclusions can you make
on the basis of your
collected observation
data?

VIII. Conclusions can be
arrived at regarding:
— What tasks were
chosen? By how many
pupils?
— Which tasks were
completed? By how
many pupils?
— Were certain chosen
tasks completed more
often than others?
— How often did pupils
request assistance?

Which children requested assistance? From whom?

— Were there differences among the three classes observed?

— What inferences can be made about the use of the resource center?

IX. Have you realized the goal for which your observations have been made? If not, can you redefine your problem more clearly and focus on different behaviors, and from a different perspective?

IX. The example as developed should allow the teachers to answer the question posed in Point 1 although alternative approaches to the problem could be developed.

X. Did you consider the role that methods of inquiry other than systematic observation – psychometric testing, controlled experimentation, or developmental histories – might play in dealing with your problem?

X. Does not pertain to the example presented.

(Boehm and Weinberg, 1977, 68–72)

Sample Recording Sheet for Observations in Resource Center

Week 1, Day 1   Date: 20-minute period

| Child | Activity selected | Frequency of requests for assistance from:★ | | | | Requests for check of completed activity |
		Teacher	Aide	Other child	Total	
Total						

★Use sign system and wait for instances of behavior to occur

(Boehm and Weinberg, 1977, 73)

Fitting the technique to the task and the task to the problem is crucial but often overlooked by enthusiastic researchers. Doing research is frequently seen to be essentially a question of collecting, processing and interpreting data. The necessary prior phase of getting a definition of the problem that provides you with challenging yet feasible research tasks is sometimes neglected, or rushed by in haste. Perhaps this is why so many retrospective accounts of research return to discuss this crucial phase of the process, for it is only when it is too late and the die has been cast that its significance is realized.

Part of the problem, as we have seen in Chapter 2, concerns the generation and creation of topics and problems. This established, the next phase is to frame the problem as a series of research tasks, which is far from easy and perhaps the phase where creativity and experience enter most strongly. It is certainly the case that it is in this phase that many of the later problems to emerge concerning the selection of methods and techniques will be determined. So, in trying to fit techniques to tasks it may be necessary to rethink the progress of the project to date, and to work back through the tasks and the way they have been defined, to the problem and the way it has been generated. Before the 'research', as a practical process, has begun, it is surprising how many things have been decided, how many options have become closed and how narrow has become the researcher's thinking. Boehm and Weinberg (1977) offer a checklist for deciding what kind of observation system to use (see p. 132), and their first question is: 'For what purpose was the system developed?' followed by the corollary question: 'Does the stated purpose match your goal?' These are perhaps obvious questions – so obvious that their significance and importance may be overlooked. There is always a temptation, at this stage in research, to choose techniques off the shelf so as to avoid the frustration and work involved in developing new ones. The trouble is that techniques may have factors built into their assumptions that make them inappropriate or distort the task to a point where it no longer relates to the initial problem. Research tends to be very effective in providing answers to the questions that no one is asking.

In interviewing there is at least the opportunity for dialogue; for people to challenge or question your questions. In observing, whether in using checklists or cameras, it is rather more tempting to let the technique become a justification in itself, and for the purpose and intention to fall from view. Perhaps this is sometimes a good thing and liberating for the research. Certainly most people will experience phases in a study where this happens, though perhaps they do not always notice it happening until the point comes to write up the study and they find themselves puzzled about the purpose of the enterprise, or engaging in fiction to explain the meaning and significance of the work. All this is natural, to be expected and an intrinsic part of the process. However, it helps to start questioning the gap between technique and task, task and question from the start; the more the dialogue can be sustained, the further the research will reach in the end.

Observing, I suggest, puts particular stress on the observer to be asking such questions. It is in this sense a technique that internalizes the interview, constantly putting the observer in the position of relating what is observed to questions that are primarily questions of meaning and intent. This is just as important for the 'qualitative' observer, who can get lost in notebooks full of inconsequential shorthand, as it is for the research technician armed with checklists and category systems.

OBSERVATION SYSTEMS

There are currently a wide variety of observation systems available for classroom use. They have been usefully summarized by Simon and Boyer (1970) and by Galton (1978). You should be warned, however, that these volumes consist of catalogues of available instruments and give little indication of the purposes to which they may be put, or of the likely meaning of the data they provide. In order to pursue such questions it is necessary to put the instruments back into a context of use, either by searching the literature for more detailed accounts of their development and application or by trying them on a pilot basis.

The checklist provided by Boehm and Weinberg (1977) provides some help in quizzing the catalogues and is reproduced here:

Checkpoints for determining the appropriateness of an observation system

Checklist   *Comment*

1 For what purpose was the system
developed?
Does the stated purpose match your
goal?

2 Are the conditions for observer
reliability met?
A: Behaviors to be viewed are
sufficiently specified so as to be:
Mutually exclusive (do not overlap
each other).
Exhaustive* (all behaviors of
concern for the given problem, can
be classified).
B: Categories are sufficiently narrow
so that two or more observers will
place an observed behavior into
the same category.
C: Is observer interpretation
necessary or not?

3 What type of system is employed?
A: Category system: every unit of
behavior observed is categorized
into one of the categories
specified.
B: Sign system: selected behavioral
units, listed beforehand, may or
may not actually be observed
during a period of time.

4 Are appropriate sampling procedures
employed?
A: The procedure for sampling
behaviors is systematic:
Time sampling: occurrence or
nonoccurrence of behaviors within

specified uniform time units.
Event sampling: event recorded
each time it occurs.

B: Is the procedure feasible?
How do you sample individuals to
be observed?
In what period of time?
Is the desired detail possible given
the number of individuals and time
units?

C: What is the coding system like?
Do tallies or codes require
memorization? If coding required,
is code indicated on the record
form?

D: Are the behaviors to be viewed
representative?
How many behaviors are to be
viewed?
Over what period of time?
Using how many subjects?

5 Are the conditions for validity met?
Are the behaviors you observe relevant to the inferences you
make?
Have sources of observer bias been eliminated?

*Optional, depending on purpose of particular observation.

(Boehm and Weinberg, 1977, 58–9)

It may also be useful to refer back to the checklist developed
by Millman at this point (see pp. 19–22), for though his list was
developed as a retrospective critical tool it raises questions about
need, market, sizes and kinds of effects, causation, audience,
durability, generalizability, statistical significance, legality/
morality/enjoyability, cost, future availability/improvements/
costs, comparative significance and overall value. Evaluators
will recognize these items as deriving from Scriven (Scriven and
Roth, 1977), and they may seem too product- and market-
oriented for some researchers. Nevertheless, the questions are
for the most part valid and useful and should not be passed by
too readily.

To return to the problem of selecting suitable observational systems for research, it may be helpful to group the maze of existing techniques. The grouping most frequently used is between checklists, or sign systems, and category systems. Checklists provide a series of items which can be recorded as present or not present in a particular classroom, usually on a time-sampling basis. They are therefore useful for making comparisons across a number of classrooms in terms of the relative presence or absence of phenomena, resources or behaviours.

Colin Hook provides some interesting examples of checklists used by teachers in different research projects. One is an attempt to record aggressive behaviour in class:

Action checklist for aggressive behaviour

	Time interval (minutes)				
Behaviour	*0*	*5*	*10*	*15*	*18*
Personal physical attack					
Taunting/ridicule					
Threatening					
Destruction of another pupil's labours					
Usurping property					
etc.					

Alternatively, the checklist could be set out as follows:

Behaviour	*No. of occurrences*
Personal physical attack	
Taunting/ridicule	
etc.	

Other examples include a checklist devised by a woodwork teacher to document pupil skills, and another used by a geography teacher attempting to evaluate a fieldwork project:

Checklist for woodworking skills

Behaviour	Satisfactory	Unsatisfactory
Chisels trench		
Saws down a line		
Uses marking gauge		
Explains what is face side and face edge		
Uses try-square		
Sharpens chisel or plane iron		
etc.		

Checklist for field excursion

Activity	Stop 1	Stop 2	Stop 3
Sketching scenery			
Examining vegetation			
Photographing scenery			
Making field notes			
Gathering samples			
Taking measurements			
Drawing sketch maps			

(Hook, 1981, 82)

Other checklists might pay attention to the availability and/or frequency of use of materials and resources (say, in art studio, science lab, or in a nursery/reception class). Alternatively it might record the frequency and occurrence of laughter or of co-operation.

Simple checklists are relatively easy to construct; more sophisticated systems do not pull items from the air but through a long period of testing select and sort them on a statistical basis. Thus an instrument like Medley and Mitzel's OScAR contains items that have been shown to reveal, on cluster or factor analysis, significant differences between classrooms in terms of 'dimensions' that are created by combining a number of single items which in themselves are not significant.

The line between checklists and category systems is not an easy one to draw. I prefer to keep the term 'category system' to refer to systems that, unlike checklists, use a relatively small number of items, each of which is more general than a typical checklist item, but which attempts to use the system to maintain some sort of more-or-less continuous record. The system you will find referred to most often is Flanders Interaction Analysis (Flanders, 1970), which is basically a ten-category system for recording teacher-pupil talk. Using the Flanders system requires the observer to code, each three seconds, what category best fits classroom talk at that time. At the end of an observation you come away with a record of the lesson in terms of a string of coded numbers which allow certain kinds of analysis of teaching style to be carried out. There are numerous variations and elaborations of the Flanders method available, many of which are to be found in Simon and Boyer (1970) and in Galton (1978).

The ten categories that form the basis of the Flanders system were derived from various theories about group leadership and productivity (i.e. learning) current in American social psychology in the mid-1940s. In Flanders' own terms the key distinction is between what he calls 'indirect' and 'direct' patterns of teacher influence, though it is not difficult to see the relationship of these terms to 'democratic' and 'authoritarian', 'dominative' and 'integrative', or other adjectives current in research at that time. In summary the categories may be described as follows:

Teacher talk

Indirect influence

1. Accepts feeling: accepts and clarifies the feeling tone of the students in a non-threatening manner. Feelings may be positive or negative. Predicting and recalling feelings are included.
2. Praises or encourages: praises or encourages student action or behaviour. Jokes that release tension, not at the expense of another individual, nodding head or saying 'uh huh?' or 'go on' are included.
3. Accepts or uses ideas of student: clarifying, building, or developing ideas or suggestions by a student. As teacher brings more of his own ideas into play, shift to category five.
4. Asks questions: asking a question about content or procedure with the intent that a student answer.

Direct influence

5. Lectures: giving facts or opinions about content or procedure; expressing his own ideas; asking rhetorical questions.
6. Gives directions: directions, commands, or orders with which a student is expected to comply.
7. Criticizes or justifies authority: statements, intended to change student behaviour from non-acceptable to acceptable pattern; bawling someone out; stating why the teacher is doing what he is doing, extreme self-reference.

Student talk

8. Student talk-response: talk by students in response to teacher. Teacher initiates the contact or solicits student statement.
9. Student talk-initiation: talk by students, which they initiate. If 'calling on' student is only to indicate who may talk next, observer must decide whether student wanted to talk. If he did, use this category.

Silence

10. Silence or confusion: pauses, short periods of silence, and periods of confusion in which communication cannot be understood by the observer.

(Flanders, 1970)

Using these categories to code each three-second interval of classroom talk generates strings of numbers as set below:

1–10	5	5	5	5	5	5	5	5	5	5
11–20	5	5	6	6	6	0	0	4	8	6
21–30	0	0	6	6	8	8	8	8	8	8
31–40	6	5	4	8	4	8	4	4	8	4
41–50	8	5	5	4	0	8	4	8	8	8
51–60	5	5	5	4	8	8	8	6	6	0
61–70	0	4	8	4	5	4	8	8	0	8
71–80	8	8	5	5	6	8	8	6	8	8
81–90	5	5	4	8	4	4	8	4	8	3
91–100	3	5	5	5	5	5	5	5	6	6

Each line represents thirty seconds of real time. Thus the first thirty-six seconds is teacher talk, followed by directions . . .

These strings of numbers may be set out in a 10 × 10 matrix by considering adjacent pairs in each string as representing co-ordinates. The following matrix was produced by taking the codes in the above table in this way. In the matrix each coded interval (except the first and last) is thus used twice, first to identify a row and second a column. For example, the string 6, 7, 10, 5, produces the pairs 6–7, 7–10, 10–5, 5– .

Category	1	2	3	4	5	6	7	8	9	10	Total
1	–	–	–	–	–	–	–	–	–	–	–
2	–	1	1	1	2	–	–	1	5	–	11
3	–	–	5	1	4	–	–	–	–	–	10
4	–	–	–	23	2	1	–	42	3	5	76
5	–	2	1	22	80	1	2	3	3	3	117
6	–	–	–	1	–	start	1	3	–	–	5
7	–	–	–	–	2	1	1	–	–	–	4
8	–	5	–	22	19	–	–	45	7	–	98
9	–	3	3	3	7	–	–	3	32	–	51
10	–	–	–	3	1	2	–	1	1	–	8
Total	–	11	10	76	117	5	4	98	51	8	380
%	–	2.9	2.6	20.0	30.8	1.3	1.1	25.8	13.4	2.1	100
%				58.7				39.2	2.1		100

Such matrices were originally intended to provide the basis for various tests of statistical significance, but they also have the advantage of providing a means for analysing teaching strategies. At its simplest this involves identifying a high scoring cell (in this case 5–5) and tracing sequences from it by locating the next highest scoring cell in the same row, then going to the row identified by the column address of that cell. Thus, in this example, to go from 5–5 to 5–4, then to row 4 where cell 4–8 leads on to row 8 . . .

Flanders' book provides a more detailed analysis of strategies in these terms but the basic principle is sketched out here. The point is that what is generally considered as a quantitative measure can be used to qualitative effect. That is to say the matrices, which are derived from measures of a kind and which may be treated statistically, are used here to produce descriptive accounts of teaching strategy that could not readily be produced by other means. We have in this sense a reverse of the procedures we saw Stake and Easley using in the previous section, where case-study material was used to generate a questionnaire survey.

OBSERVATION FOR DESCRIPTION

It is not easy to think of the right term to place in opposition to systematic observation. The obvious term, unsystematic observation, is not accurate except in a very limited sense and carries prejudicial overtones. Broadly what I am concerned with here is observational techniques that remain close to the natural observations made by teachers and others as part of their routine work. A lot of this observation goes on; pupils observe teachers, teachers observe pupils; teaching practice supervisors, inspectors, school psychologists and heads all have a considerable investment in observation. They tend not to make their methods and techniques explicit, though increasingly there is pressure on them to do so.

What I am concerned with here are ways of strengthening this kind of 'natural' observation rather than introducing add-on systems or replacements – which is what I would argue techniques like Flanders do.

One method increasingly used is to tape record or videotape lessons in order to provide the basis for extending or elaborating 'natural' observation. This offers some of the same understanding that slow motion and stop-frame analyses of sporting highlights provide for the enthusiast. Experience suggests though that the method on its own is inadequate and that techniques need to be brought to bear in order to understand this new reality. One useful suggestion is provided by David Ireland who, with Thomas Russell, attempted to start teachers researching their own teaching by having them audiotape some of their lessons. They suggest using a method of pattern analysis to begin making sense of what they discovered:

Pattern analysis is a technique for looking at what happens in classrooms. One of its most constructive applications is its use to provide 'feedback' which is otherwise not readily available to teachers. Pattern analysis is an 'open-ended' technique, rather than a preconceived set of categories for analysis. It is amenable to a variety of different points of view and is probably most useful to teachers who have already identified particular aspects of their teaching which they wish to examine.

Some examples of patterns

A. To every student response, the teacher replies with the phrase, 'O.K., very good.'
B. When the teacher proposes an idea, the students elaborate it.
C. When the teacher asks students to read a book, students may choose from several titles.
D. Virtually all questions are asked by the teacher.
E. When the teacher records responses on the board, the responses are recorded in precisely the language used by the students.
F. When students propose an idea, the teacher elaborates it.
G. When students make no response, the teacher never waits more than three seconds before speaking again.
H. After the teacher speaks, a student speaks; then the teacher speaks again, then a student, and so on.
I. The teacher often sits behind the desk when speaking to the entire class.
J. To every student response, the teacher replies by saying 'Yes, . . ., but . . .'
K. Students usually wait to speak until the teacher calls on them.

Pattern analysis: the basic technique

1. Tape record a class, and then transcribe word for word a small portion of the tape. (For example, five minutes of the class, or enough of the tape to fill three or four pages of paper.)
2. Read through the transcript, looking for patterns . . . regularities of behaviour, forms of interaction which occur over and over again.

State these patterns in descriptive terms. It is important to avoid interpretive language which goes beyond the data and assumes knowledge of thoughts and intentions. We try to avoid interpretive language because it introduces values and judgments about what is happening.

For example, if a teacher has a regular way of using words of praise, say what that regular way is, but do not assume that the praise was intended or that the words actually had the effect of praise on students.

In short, at this stage it is enough to describe behaviour patterns. Interpretation of patterns is a second stage in the use of pattern analysis.

A note on recording: It's best to use a cassette tape recorder with an automatic level control. Locate the recorder closer to students than to the teacher . . . the teacher's voice is always the loudest. Try the recorder when the classroom is empty to make sure it is working; it's very disappointing to make the effort of recording, only to find that the tape is blank or inaudible.

(Ireland and Russell, 1978, 21)

This approach may be used in a number of ways. Anyone with an interest in socio-linguistics will find in the examples given here starting points that might be readily translated into detailed and systematic research studies. On the other hand the level and style of analysis suggested may be sustained and a closer grip kept on the immediate professional issues of teaching, learning and classroom organization.

The same is generally true of videotape recording. In the early days of video use in classroom research the technique was applied to problems that remained from previous research. That is to say, videotape made it possible to solve some of the long-standing problems of inter-observer reliability, of selectivity and of validity that remained from previous decades of research effort (for example in the work of Biddle and Adams, 1971, and Kounin, 1970).

Other problems were of course created by videotape, or at least made worse, namely those involving the reactivity of the subjects and interference effects stemming from the intrusiveness of the technology.

Recently, however, researchers have begun using videotape in ways that are more suited to its own potential strengths and weaknesses, rather than using it to solve other people's problems. One major development has been in the making of documentary films (for example in the *Kingswood* series mentioned previously); in research, video has been used not only to record, but for its interactive effect: that is to say, making virtues out of the very things that in conventional terms appear weaknesses. Hull and Rudduck, for example, have used videotape to record discussion-based teaching in a school where it is an established approach in order to replay it to children in

schools where such an approach is being introduced as an innovation (see Rudduck, 1981). Such a process short-circuits to some extent the intermediate process of interpretation, and creates a novel role for the researcher as a manager of the research process rather than as solely responsible for 'doing research'.

Once the step is taken to invoke and involve the interpretative response of others, rather than seeing this as essentially the researcher's task, then a range of possibilities opens up. Photographs, for example, long unused in observational research because of the problems of subjectivity and bias associated with the taking and processing of pictures, provide a more acceptable stimulus once selectivity becomes part of the subject of the research. The two photographs opposite, for example, were taken in fairly rapid succession. They show just how selective is the process. A slight shift in angle, the inclusion or exclusion of contextual information, the choice of one split-second rather than another provide similar pictures open to very different interpretations.

This very weakness of the photograph as data can be turned to a strength when it is used to elicit responses or to communicate complex messages. Often in applied studies what has to be communicated to people is not a processed and unambiguous set of findings, but rather some portrayal of an event. If, for example, you are asked to evaluate a conference or a course, or to look at a novel teaching programme, part of the task may be to replay events to the people involved to get them thinking and talking reflectively. In this kind of situation the photograph may well have a place and a role to play. What is important about the picture is determined, in part at least, by what people say about it. Pat Templin provides a diagram to help guide this process (p. 144).

The ambiguities that are intrinsic to the visual record are a consequence of the complexity of information that images contain. At the same time photographs, films and videotape are the result of a series of selections that derive from the nature of recording systems and the actions of the recorded. Erickson and Wilson argue that, in viewing visual and audiovisual records it is important to bear this selection and editorial process in mind:

It is important to keep in mind that any kind of documentary is essentially a case study. No documentary case study, whether

Collecting the data

Start here

Talk with clients, program staff, audiences

Select sampling method

Select instances to photograph

Develop program issues

Select photographer(s)

Discover concerns of constituents, audiences, information needed

Obtain permissions to photograph

Negotiate access with camera

Begin taking many pictures

Photograph mapping shots, detail and close-up shots

Select representative pictures, focus issues, topics

Go back, photointerview, interview, observe, rephotograph, gather verbatim data, repeat

Validate, confirm attempt to disconfirm story, issues

Rephotograph, repeat process

Assemble photos narrative materials for report

(Templin, 1979; see also Templin, 1982)

reported through the medium of print or through an audiovisual medium, is a full account of what actually happened in everyday life. All case studies are highly selective accounts, and any selection from life reduces its complexity and involves an interpretive point of view. Selection of what is to be included in the account focuses the attention of the viewer or reader on what the film editor or writer considers to be the key aspects of the happenings portrayed. The key aspects are foregrounded, while other aspects are backgrounded. In the written case study, this is done through variation in descriptive scope, detail and emphasis. It is done in the audiovisual document by variation in camera angles, framing, pointing of the microphone, and in the cutting and sequencing of the shots. What is judged salient and given emphasis in the document depends on the editor's descriptive theory of the events being described. In edited documentaries editorial selection points the viewer directly to the main message of the film or tape and to interpretive patterns for viewing and for reflecting on what is there to be seen and heard. Having one's visual and auditory attention directed one way or another is an intrinsic part of the experience of viewing edited documents.

(Erickson and Wilson, 1982, 6)

While acknowledging that audiovisual media have been used to collect information in the context of experimental studies, Erickson and Wilson, in what is one of the most useful surveys of the field, declare their preference for audiovisual techniques as an extension of participant observation and they suggest projects which lend themselves to this approach:

Audiovisual documentation involves the recording of the finely shaded details of everyday life in a setting. The record permits the researcher and the researcher's audience various kinds of vicarious 'revisiting' at later points in time. Because settings of social life are so complex and their details are so numerous, the ability to revisit an audiovisual record enables us to compensate for our limited human information processing capacities and to discover, after the fact, new aspects of meaning and organization that we did not realize at first. Audiovisual documentation and analysis is a research procedure that is essentially similar in its underlying logic to that of participant observational fieldwork. Indeed, as we will argue here, the best way to do audiovisual documentation research is to do it in conjunction with fieldwork. Consequently the ensuing discussion of methods presented here resembles very much the discussions found in the standard literature of ethnography and participant observation.

Issues of substance that might be addressed by audiovisual documentation and analysis are basically the same as those classically
considered by fieldwork researchers in education. Topics especially
appropriate for study by audiovisual documentation are those
involving the conduct and organization of face to face interaction . . .
Other kinds of topics in educational research that have been studied by
means of audiovisual documentation are:

1. Relationships between federal and state mandates and building
   and classroom level implementation, for a variety of issues such
   as racial desegregation, gender equity, teacher centers for the
   improvement of instruction, and the implementation of special
   education service delivery systems, including the natural history
   of referral decisions from their origin in the classroom
   experience of the teacher through the development of an indivi-
   dualized instruction plant for the student.
2. The role of the principal, in relation to school staff, students and
   the school community.
3. The implementation of a curriculum innovation in subject
   matter content (e.g., social studies) or in the reconstruction of
   social relationships in teaching and learning (open education,
   direct instruction).
4. Peer relationships among teachers involved in planning and
   implementing district-wide changes.
5. Classroom teaching, considered from a variety of aspects, and
   for a variety of purposes (classrooms are the settings that have
   been documented audiovisually most frequently in educational
   research).
6. Illustration and analysis of particular teaching techniques.

In sum, audiovisual documentation and analysis is useful in
collecting records that have a documentary interest and function
analogous to those of the written records studied by historians.
Audiovisual documentation and analysis is also useful in discovering
new insights about the organization of everyday life in educational
settings – new perspectives on phenomena that may have been overlooked because of their subtlety and their familiarity to those closest to
them.

(Erickson and Wilson, 1982, 40–1)

Erickson and Wilson, Templin, and Dabbs (all 1982), and the
various authors who contribute to Wagner's (1979) book have
many useful suggestions to make about the uses that can be
made of audiovisual records in social research. One area that is
sometimes overlooked, however, is that of presentation. Often

innovative projects are in the end reduced to using still photographs in order to illustrate a text, not because the research itself is limited to this device, but because the available channels of dissemination are restricted in their character and conventions. Perhaps as a result some texts overlook the kinds of presentation possibilities inherent in the media. Erickson and Wilson offer some valuable advice about showing films and tapes recorded in a research context to groups of teachers:

2.221 Choosing a place to start and stop

Decide in advance when to begin a segment to be shown and when to end it. The segment itself is usually a connected series of events: one whole discourse topic in a lesson, one whole round in a game, the whole sequence in which a staff meeting is called to order and begun, the whole wind-up phase in a parent-administrator conference. Usually no more than two to three minutes of minimally edited footage can be viewed continuously without viewers' overload setting in. The selection of an appropriate place to start and stop is a very important decision. A common mistake of people showing unedited footage is to try to show too much of it at once. The maxim of the architect Mies van der Rohe applies here: 'Less is more.'

2.222 Describing contexts outside the tape

It is important to tell before the actual screening or after it, what needs to be known more generally about the school or community setting in which the documented events occurred. Often it is also important to tell what happened in the immediate scene before and after the strip that is shown, and to tell some salient points of contrast between what the viewer can see and what happens at other times in the same kind of scene or in other kinds of scenes of everyday life in the school and community.

2.223 Orienting to important features in the segment

It is helpful to point out in advance the arrangement of people and objects in space, the most significant actors in the events that will be viewed, and a description of the action sequence to be seen (one that describes it as a whole and points to salient strategic moves within it). The description of sequential and strategic relationships among the actors in the event anticipates for the audience what is about to happen, focusing their expectations, just as shot sequencing and camera angles do in highly edited documentary films. In addition, this kind of commentary by a presenter provides an analytic frame of reference for the viewers, placing in the foreground some of the key relationships between one occurrence and another.

Key relationships may be those of sequencing or of simultaneity. Here, for example, is a helpful presenter comment about sequencing: 'Watch for the student's way of answering the teacher; each time he or she asked a question the students answered in chorus rather than in unison.' Comments about the simultaneity might be as follows: 'Notice that as the principal turned in place and opened the faculty meeting by announcing the agenda, all but three teachers turned in their chairs and oriented posturally to the principal in the same moment in which he or she was turning and beginning to speak. Those teachers who were oriented to the principal stopped speaking in side conversations as the principal began to speak. The three teachers who did not stop talking with each other at that moment can be seen on the left of the screen, sitting together. Later in the meeting these were the teachers who disagreed with what the principal proposed to the faculty.'

Sometimes in using minimally edited film or videotape for teaching purposes you may want the audience to induce organizing properties rather than point them out yourself in advance. In that case you need to provide some framing for their induction: 'In this lesson segment see how many different types of teacher questions you can identify.' 'In this segment from a school staff meeting see if you can identify, according to nonverbal cues, the group of teachers that will later agree with what the principal has said, and the group that will later in the meeting disagree with what has been said.' Some kind of framing is necessary, even in an inductive approach to viewing. It is not enough simply to say 'Look for whatever interests you.' With that loose a frame you get discussion that wanders all over the place.

2.224 Showing the complete segment

a. *Playing the segment of interest all the way through without stopping.* The presenter may point occasionally to the screen as a way of fore-grounding key aspects of the events being shown. Usually one needs to begin showing the segment at least 10 seconds before the phenomena of special interest will begin to appear. This allows the viewers time to get involved in the sequential flow of the action, as they would be involved while watching a continuous showing of a highly edited film. Usually it is effective to continue showing at least 10 seconds after the action has moved on past the phenomena of interest. This enables viewers to have a beginning sense of the

contrast between the phenomena of interest and those events that
happened just after them.

b. *Replaying the segment of interest.* Here the presenter may rewind all
Here the presenter may rewind all the way back to the point first
shown the viewers. Or the presenter may replay only key
segments of action. The presenter may stop the film or tape
occasionally and intersperse comments. The presenter may replay
a brief segment repeatedly. When stopping and starting it is often
wise to rewind slightly ahead of the movements to which viewers
are to attend most carefully. This gives viewers a chance to
anticipate what they are about to see by getting acquainted with the
flow of action. Telling the viewers what to look for and listen for in
the replay can precede the replay itself and can also accompany it,
as the presenter occasionally points to the screen and/or 'talks over'
the action as it is being shown.

2.225 Moving on to the next segment

The presenter recycles steps 2–4 above.

2.226 Discussion after showing

Standard techniques for leading discussion apply here. The leader is
wise not to point out too soon details he or she already knows about,
but that the audience didn't see yet. Push the audience to look for
evidence in the film for assertions they are making, remembering that
your reviewing and prior training enables you to know more about
what's in the film or tape than the audience does. Try to get them to
look closely, too, but do so with patience. Questions should arise
about what actually happened. Divergent opinions should emerge
about what something meant. That is a good point to replay the
relevant section for yet another look. In general, remember that in
edited footage the interpretive framing is medium–intrinsic —
contained in the form of shooting and editing. In viewing minimally
edited footage, interpretive framing must be constructed by you and
the audience through demonstration and discussion. Minimally
edited visual material cannot be looked at passively. It must be viewed
actively, chewed on, and digested.

(Erickson and Wilson, 1982, 51–2)

Intraviews

While the interview is based on the assumption that it takes two
to tell the truth, the intraview hinges for its effect on the power

of introspection. I have included in this section those techniques that depend on the researcher using his or her own experience and subjectivity as the key instrument. The problem is essentially one of being objective about what is essentially subjective – not so impossible a task as it might seem, but one which may draw the researcher to traditions of thought in the arts rather than in the sciences.

In some respects much research data already exists in the system. People keep diaries, schools (in Britain at least) keep log books and, in the US, yearbooks. There are school magazines, notice boards, timetables, staff documents, letters and circulars to parents, pupil records. All contain material which may give insight into the individual's experience of school.

Finding such documents is one thing, stimulating their creation is another. Attempts to organize pupils in keeping diaries have been both highly successful and virtual failures. Some of the successes have become literary works or popular fiction (Bel Kaufman's *Up the Down Staircase* and Herb Kohl's *36 Children*); others have become research classics (Royston Lambert's *The Hothouse Society*, for example, which consists almost entirely of letters written by children in residential schools).

It is difficult to give advice on how to collect and use such material, though it is important to try, where possible, to integrate diary accounts with interviews, other documents (Bel Kaufman has some excellent examples), or observational data. Mary Louise Holly has provided a useful handbook for teachers on 'keeping a professional diary' which includes some examples (Holly, 1984).

School log books are not always easily accessible though many from old (or closed) schools find their way into local libraries or public record offices. Ronald Blythe includes extracts from the school log book in his study of an English village, *Akenfield:*

1900

I, Florence T. Spurling, this day commenced duties as Head Mistress of the Akenfield Mixed School. I found the children very backward in every respect. No single standard knew their work.

Taught the whole school a new song – *The old folks at home.*
The average attendance is 43.2. Commenced the Royal Copy Books.
Gave special attention to Arithmetic.
(March) Owing to the very cold East winds a large amount of sickness
prevails.
The children went to church for Intercession at 11.15 (The Boer War).
Peter and Nellie Whittle were kept at home two days this week to go
stone-picking with their mother.
Government Report: 'There has been a change of teachers here and the
Managers are setting an example to the county by their sensible
policy. A handsome gift for the improvement of classroom accom-
modation has been made by a lady. Everything has improved here.'

1901

Government Report: 'The infants have been kindly and con-
scientiously taught by Miss Spurling but their classroom should be
enlarged without delay. I have found it unhealthily crowded several
times. An excellent room for entertainments could be produced by
partitioning-off a classroom – and villages are generally admitted to be
in need of amusements if the exodus to the towns is to be arrested.'
Alice Tilney, being 13, left school on Monday to go into service.
Charles Deering was caned (four stripes) for repeated disobedience
and the Brown brothers were caned (one stripe each) for stealing
apples. All the big boys were caned on Wednesday for throwing
stones at men working in the opposite field. John Marriage was
expelled (November) for refusing to obey me. But he apologized the
next morning, so I allowed him to come to school again. I
administered corporal punishment to William Brown (December) for
insubordination.

1902

Eight children are still away with the water-pox.
Average attendance, 72 per cent.
Government Report: 'Sound foundations are being laid here.'

1904

I have caned James Williams again for misbehaving himself. He is a
bad boy and takes easy advantage. His mother refused to send him in
the afternoon and sent instead an insolent message. He is the only boy
to receive corporal punishment in this school for 3 months.
83 children are present. H.M.I.s have awarded the school the Highest
Grant.

It is impossible to teach here as one would like. I have to work Standards III, IV, V and VI in different subjects in the same room.

1906

14 children have received notice that they cannot attend this school after Friday next because of its overcrowded state.

1907

Empire Day (30th May) was celebrated in school today. Her Ladyship kindly lent 20 flags and the children were taught to salute the Union Jack. Lessons were given on the Union Jack and the 'Growth and Extent of the British Empire'. Several patriotic songs were sung, and the afternoon was spent in organised games. Three selected compositions on 'Empire Day' were dispatched to one of the colonies.

1910

The dimensions of the two classrooms are 32 ft × 22 ft, and 22 ft × 17 ft. There are 72 children and no lavatories.

1911

The jumble sale raised £5 towards a school piano.

(Blythe, 1972, 168–9)

Recently reports from HMI have become available, though it remains to be seen how informative or useful these are likely to be, or how much they become used. If the following example, written in the 1950s on a school that has since closed, is anything to go by, such reports may provide valuable documents in recording the physical conditions of schools but be less valuable in describing the curriculum in action:

This small County Primary School now has only 37 children in attendance. For some years, senior children have attended ———— Secondary Modern School, about two miles distant. ———— is a scattered village and some of the children walk nearly two miles to School; children of the new estate at the far side of the village attend ———— County Primary School.

The premises occupy a small, rather isolated site. There are two classrooms, two cloakrooms and a kitchen. The School is without mains water and electricity services, but both are available in the vicinity, and it is understood that they will be brought to the School shortly. Meanwhile, water is obtained from a hand-pump in the playground; it is conveyed to the kitchen by pipe-line, but is carried to the cloakrooms where the children use portable enamelled bowls for washing. There is no artificial lighting at present. Better use could be made of the natural lighting in the larger classroom by a re-arrangement of the class; this is recommended. Heating is by an open fire and a stove which maintains a radiator system in both rooms. The premises are decorated internally in light, pleasant colours.

The major part of the playground was surfaced early this term, but the small paddock, which forms part of the School site, is in poor condition and unfit for use. Pail sanitation facilities, which are well kept, continue to be unavoidable. Along the front of the School buildings is a wide garden-border flanked by a narrow paved extension of the playground. This border and other small plots about the site are maintained by the children who need no longer be separated from their garden by the short strip of iron railings erected in very different circumstances many years ago.

The kitchen was built at one end of the premises in 1945. Meals, of necessity in present conditions, are cooked on an iron stove or on oil-stoves. Almost all the children stay to dinner. Dining-tables are erected in the larger classroom, but some table-desks, suitably covered, are also used. Food is served in the other room and conveyed by selected boys and girls to the tables. The arrangements work smoothly and the children enjoy their meals. Although washing facilities are not easy to organise, the children wash before the meal and use individual towels provided by their parents.

The Head Mistress was appointed to her present post in 1953. She had previously been on the staff as an assistant since 1941, and had taken the special one-year course of training for serving teachers in 1949–50. For some time, the permanent assistant qualified teacher, also appointed in 1953, has been absent on sick leave and the date of her return to duty is uncertain. Meanwhile, a qualified supply teacher is in charge of the Infant class.

There are 19 children, aged five to seven, in the lower class where much importance is attached to work which aims to give the children the basic skills. On the whole, satisfactory progress is made by most of the children in reading, writing and simple number work. Group reading is well organised and the older children show promise in their written work, but they would benefit from more opportunities to write spontaneously on topics which appeal to them. Their news writing is creditable. For number work rather more, and more varied teaching equipment is needed. Some of the physical and musical activities are conducted in the classroom which has an extension loud

speaker from the battery wireless set in the Junior classroom. Broad-
casts to Schools, intended for Infants, are used profitably. Other
music and dancing lessons have to be taken in the larger room where a
piano is available; unfortunately, this causes disturbance to the Junior
class. The Infants do a good range of simple exercises in Art, mainly
with suitable paints, and a good deal of useful handwork is done; the
part which clay-modelling might take in handwork lessons merits
attention. Similarly, the value of teaching aids such as a well-managed
nature table, a library corner and a classroom shop, might also be
considered.

During the period of her staffing difficulty, the Head Mistress has
assumed charge of the Junior class, which now numbers 18 children
aged seven to eleven. Previously she was responsible for the Infant
class. The upper class falls naturally into three clearly defined groups.
In view of the widely differing attainments of the children in the
respective groups rather more group work is needed in most subjects.
One-third of the children are markedly backward or retarded and
their attainments in reading and written work are low; in two or three
cases there are special reasons, beyond the control of the teacher, for
this condition. The smaller, middle group consists of younger
children, recently promoted from the Infant class, who show much
promise and need only normal opportunities to make progress. The
upper group makes a good impression; the girls, who predominate,
show marked ability and they might be extended considerably in their
work. All the children have a good attitude towards their work and
the more able boys and girls are clearly anxious to do well. In tests
conducted during the Inspection the older children did creditable
work.

Among present needs for this class are more definite schemes of
work in History and Geography to provide for the three or four years
which children have to spend in it. More emphasis might be placed on
suitable free written work and a more ambitious programme might be
arranged in Art and handwork. At present, work in the information
subjects is heavily based on certain textbooks and makes too little
demand on the children; individual work-books would make possible
more factual written work. The able children would also profit from
opportunities to use simple books of a reference character and to
record the results of their investigations in their own books. In
English lessons, the writing of diaries and original stories is a
commendable feature, but formal exercise work is over-emphasised.
Pattern-making exercises in Art are creditable, but the children's
illustrative work, executed with the aid of coloured pencils or
crayons, in their nature note-books suggests the need for more
attention to be given to neat sketching exercises. The contribution

which handwork, in various media, can make to the expression work done in History, Geography and Religious Instruction might also receive attention.

The newly-surfaced playground has considerably improved conditions for Physical Education: the need now is for a better grass playing-space for the more vigorous organised games. Music is given much attention, and the children sing a wide repertoire of appropriate songs with enjoyment. They also show satisfaction in their dancing.

The Head Mistress is facing her many difficulties with courage. She contrives to give the children a happy environment in which it is evident that even the less gifted child knows he is wanted for his own sake. For this, much credit is due to her.

School timetables, while not strictly intraviews, are a valuable source for curriculum analysis, especially in the secondary school, and indeed there are sophisticated techniques available for timetable analysis in terms of use of space/time/ staffing and resources (e.g. Johnson, 1980). Combined with budgets and lists of stock (particularly textbooks) and examination syllabuses, such information can be used to get an insight into ways in which organizational and curricular issues connect, and sometimes clash. Such detailed case studies are, however, relatively rare.

Summary

In this chapter I have indicated a wide range of techniques that might be drawn on in carrying out a research project. These techniques have not been discussed in great detail, nor do they comprise an exclusive list of available research tools. It is important not to lose sight of the intent and purpose of the project, or to design complex and demanding research or evaluation studies that might drain energy better put to other purposes. In educational research, perhaps more than in any other area of social and human research, the context of use should never be subsumed to questions of a technical kind. The temptation is to let technical questions displace educational questions. It is a temptation that needs to be resisted.

5 Processing research data and presenting research reports

Processing research data

Given the limited scope of this book this section will inevitably be restricted in its content. The processing of survey findings, of observational data and of audio-visual recordings are topics for which it is necessary to turn to other sources where more detail is available.[1]

More generally, a major consideration in applied studies is the circulation of draft reports, of segments of reports, of extracts from data and of short preliminary statements in order both to obtain clearance and to gauge initial responses. Transcripts of interviews, descriptive observations made in classrooms, portrayals of schools, proof sheets of photographs, roughcut film and lightly edited videotape are all frequently shown to those portrayed by them as part of the process of clearing confidentiality procedures such as those described in Chapter 2. Although the principal purpose of this process is one of obtaining consent, it is rarely simply so, for when prompted people are usually more than willing to offer comments, further data or their own analysis. This raises the problem of what to do with such material. Sometimes (for example with interview

---

1 For measurement data see Borg and Gall (1979), ch. 19, or any similar educational research text. For a more challenging view, though one that requires some research and statistical background, see Tukey (1977). For a valuable cautionary note which remains valid see Stinnett (1957). For observational data see the valuable annotated bibliography in Hammersley and Atkinson (1983), and for case-study research see Hamilton *et al.* (1977) and Simons (1980). For visual material see Collier (1967), Wagner (1979), Erickson and Wilson (1982), Templin (1982) and Shoemaker (1982). For possibilities outside the orthodox and conventional see Smith (1981a, 1981b).

transcripts) the clarifications and reformulations that people offer can replace the original statement. Sometimes (for example with transcripts of classroom interaction) it is both necessary and desirable to retain the original transcript intact, but people's comments on it can be used to identify critical incidents, and may be further used as a secondary source. (See, for instance, the Ford Teaching Booklet *The Tins*, assembled by Clem Adelman, which consists of a segment of classroom transcript, the comments made on it by the teacher, the pupils' comments, and the teacher's comments on seeing the pupils' comments.)

Overall, if the kind of analysis you are working towards is one consisting of lists of issues, then these can be used as a means of organizing and selecting material. The pursuit of an issues analysis (which is common in applied research) makes for a different approach from that commonly taken in social science studies, where the pursuit is for generalizations which in turn leads the researcher towards statistical models (even in qualitative studies). Generally speaking, issues are most effectively identified by following any discrepancies that emerge: within the statements made by one person, between what people say and what they do, or between policy and practice. Sometimes these will be large-scale discrepancies – for example a school that has a policy of mixed-ability teaching apparently implementing forms of disguised streaming. They may be discrepancies at the level of classroom practice (for example, 'The Tins' episode referred to above). Or they may be significant discontinuities encapsulated in a single utterance. In a study of advisers and inspectors, I observed a course at the end of which one of the heads made an impromptu speech of thanks to the inspectors who had organized the course, saying, 'How lucky we are to have two such nice people as inspectors.' This innocent remark became the key to an extensive line of enquiry which pursued the interrelation of personal and professional roles.

At a practical level, organizing material as issues emerge is a facet of the research process which will be handled very differently by individuals. Some prefer to use categorization systems of one kind or another – filing systems, making notes on file cards and sticking them on (large!) walls, using blackboards to revise and reorganize accumulating ideas, or, increasingly, making use of computerized systems. Others simply store and organize material in their heads.

The use of computer-based systems is an obvious future line of development, especially as expert-systems become available which allow for the accumulation of extensive records in particular knowledge fields. For the present, however, the main applications have been in the use of word-processing techniques to maintain indexes which allow reanalysis of, say, interview transcripts or of classroom interactions stored on discs (Tripp, 1983b), and in the use of computer systems to maintain research networks (Bell, 1981). Computing has of course become a standard technique in quantitative studies, and one project in particular has attempted to use the technology to bring about the kinds of shift in the nature of access to research which has formed a theme of this book. The Scottish Data Archive set up by MacPherson and his colleagues in Edinburgh consists of a regular survey of Scottish school leavers. It is open to almost anyone to obtain access to the data archive via computer terminals, and in addition to 'piggy back' on the regular surveys by adding their questions to the core of questions which forms the central structure of the archive. Perhaps more than any other large-scale research study this demonstrates the degree of democracy that can be engineered with modern facilities and equipment.

Presenting research reports

For most users the primary source of research is through specialist journals. Secondary sources might include textbooks, review articles, the popular media and professional courses of one kind or another.

One source of access to the technical literature is by browsing in the current periodicals section of a library and by scanning contents pages of journals. If you do so it soon becomes clear that journals vary considerably in their style of presentation and in the kind and range of content they carry. This is a somewhat haphazard though surprisingly productive procedure. If you want to approach a topic more systematically, or to pursue it more thoroughly, there is an extensive infrastructure to help you to do so. A good example is the *Current Index of Journals in Education* which provides an extensive subject-based catalogue of journal articles. An extract from a recent edition gives some idea of the kind of coverage and range of the index:

Advanced Placement Programs

Extending Advanced Placement Opportunities to the Business Student. *Journal of Business Education*; v57 n1 p31–32 Oct 1981.
EJ 250 816

Advertising

Popularity of Self-Help Counseling Tapes as an Index of Community Needs. *Journal of Counseling Psychology*; v28 n5 p445–50 Sep 1981
EJ 250 903

Advisory Committees

Adult Continuing Education and the Federal Advisory Committees. *Lifelong Learning: The Adult Years*; v5 n1 p8–9, 25 Sep 1981
EJ 250 796

The Role of the Student on a Committee for Academic Reform. *Liberal Education*; v67 n2 p124–28 Sum 1981.   EJ 251 205

What Should Be the Federal Role in Education? A Question for the Intergovernmental Advisory Council on Education. *Action in Teacher Education*; v3 n2–3 p9–12 Sum-Fall 1981.   EJ 251 665

Affective Behavior

The Affective Response of Down's Syndrome Infants to a Repeated Event. *Child Development*; v52 n2 p745–48 Jun 1981.   EJ 251 380

Affirmative Action

"Reverse Discrimination" in Employment. Judicial Treatment of Affirmative Action Programmes in the United States. *International Labour Review*; v120 n4 p453–72 Jul-Aug 1981.   EJ 250 813

African Languages

A Socio-Linguistic Typology of Language Contact in Nigeria: The Role of Translation. *Babel (International Journal of Translation)*; v27 n1 p9–16 1981.   EJ 251 166

African Primary Science Programme

Primary Science Curriculum Development in Africa – Strategies, Problems and Prospects with Particular Reference to the African Primary Science Programme. *European Journal of Science Education*; v3 n3 p259–69 Jul-Sep 1981.   EJ 251 564

Age Differences

Development of Ability to Process Syntactic Structures in Expanded Discourse. *Perceptual and Motor Skills*; v53 n1 p36–38 Aug 1981.
EJ 250 683

Lateral Preference Behaviors in Preschool Children and Young Adults. *Child Development*; v52 n2 p443–50 Jun 1981.   EJ 251 336

How Adolescents Approach Decisions: Changes over Grades Seven to Twelve and Policy Implications. *Child Development*; v52 n2 p538–44 Jun 1981.   EJ 251 348

Selective Imitation of Same-Age, Older, and Younger Peer Models. *Child Development*; v52 n2 p717–20 Jun 1981.   EJ 251 373

Does Recognition Memory Improve with Age? *Journal of Experimental Child Psychology*; v32 n2 p343–53 Oct 1981. EJ 251 428

Imagery and Learning: Item Recognition and Associative Recall *Journal of Educational Psychology*; v73 n2 p164–73 Apr 1981.
EJ 251 739

Age Groups

Social Participation of Preschool Children in Same- versus Mixed-Age Groups. *Child Development*; v52 n2 p644–50 Jun 1981.
EJ 251 361

Aggression

The Fantasy-Reality Distinction in Televised Violence: Modifying Influences on Children's Aggression. *Journal of Research in Personality*; v15 n3 p323–30 Sep 1981.   EJ 250 836

Bobo Clown Aggression in Childhood: Environment, Not Genes. *Journal of Research in Personality*; v15 n3 p331–42 Sep 1981.
EJ 250 837

Dynamics of Hostile Aggression: Influence of Anger, Hurt Instructions, and Victim Pain Feedback. *Journal of Research in Personality*; v15 n3 p343–58 Sep 1981.   EJ 250 838

Empathy and Stress: How They Affect Parental Aggression. *Social Work*; v26 n5 p383–89 Sep 1981.   EJ 250 890

Air Conditioning Equipment

Ventilation Cooling: An Old Solution to New Problems. Part 2: The Equipment. *American School and University*; v54 n1 p42–44 Sep 1981.   EJ 251 084

Algorithms

Even Perfect Numbers: An Update. *Mathematics Teacher*; v74 n6 p460–63 Sep 1981.   EJ 251 484

Magic Cubes: A Total Experience. *Mathematics Teacher*; v74 n6 p464–72, 492 Sep 1981.   EJ 251 485

A Variation on a Very Familiar Algorithm. *Mathematics Teacher*, v74 n6 p474–75, 490 Sep 1981.   EJ 251 486

A Review of Monte Carlo Tests of Cluster Analysis. *Multivariate Behavioral Research*; v16 n3 p379–407 Jul 1981.   EJ 251 724

Alienation

Marital Status, Happiness, and Anomia. *Journal of Marriage and the Family*; v43 n3 p643–49 Aug 1981.   EJ 250 878

Alpha Feedback Training

Alpha Biofeedback Conditioning and Retarded Subjects. *Education*; v101 n4 p389–94 Sum 1981.   EJ 251 447

(*CIJE*, 14(1), 1982)

The *CIJE* also includes abstracts which provide more detail as well as classifying the article in terms of a set of descriptors which indicate the way in which it is filed in the ERIC retrieval system:

EJ 251 760   TM 506 396
Evaluating Evaluation Methods. Smith, Nick L. *Studies in Educational Evaluation*; v7 n2 p173–81 1981 (Reprint: UMI).
Descriptors: ★Efficiency; ★Evaluation Methods; ★Methods Research.
Identifiers: ★Conceptual Analysis; ★Empirical Analysis; Evaluation Utilization.
New perspectives on evaluation methodology have been drawn from other disciplines such as law, casework and journalism. Empirical and conceptual tests to assess the practical utility of alternative perspectives of the evaluation process, and criteria for judging their adequacy are addressed. (Author/AEF)

EF 251 761   TM 506 397
The Implications of Intra-Program Placement Decisions for the Understanding and Improvement of Schooling. Hanson, Ralph A.; And Others. *Studies in Educational Evaluation*; v7 n2 p193–210 1981 (Reprint: UMI).
Descriptors: Academic Achievement; Bilingual Education; Educational Practices; Elementary Education; English (Second Language); ★Grouping (Instructional Purposes); ★Outcomes of Education; ★Performance Factors; Research Methodology; Spanish Speaking; Student Placement.

A study of Spanish-speaking elementary school students enrolled in an English as a second language program revealed a significant relationship between pupil placement status and subsequent student achievement. Methods and findings relevant to identifying schooling effects and linking these to school practices, and study of bilingual programs are presented. (AEF)

EJ 251 762   TM 506 398
High School Science as Viewed by College Students in Israel. Tamir, Pinchas; Amir, Ruth. *Studies in Educational Evaluation*; v7 n2 p211–25 1981 (Reprint: UMI).
Descriptors: Biology; Chemistry; College Freshmen; *College Preparation; *College School Cooperation; *College Science; Foreign Countries; Higher Education; Physics; *Secondary School Science; Student Attitudes.
Identifiers: Israel.
A questionnaire was administered to first-year biology, physics and chemistry students in an Israeli university to assess their views on the nature of the contribution made by their high school courses to college achievement. Results indicate that high school curriculum influences attitudes, knowledge retention, expectations, and achievement in college. (AEF)

Urban Education (UD)

EJ 251 763   UD 508 663
Constituting Ethnic Phenomenon: An Account from the Perspective of Immigrant Women. Ng, Roxanna. *Canadian Ethnic Studies*; v13 n1 p97–108 1981.
Descriptors: *Ethnicity; *Females; Foreign Countries; *Immigrants; Indians; Whites.
Identifiers: Canada.
Focuses on immigrant women in Canada, and examines ethnicity as an observable phenomenon. Argues that ethnicity arises upon immigrants' arrival, and becomes a means by which people are organized in relation to the productive and political processes of the society. (Author/DA)

EJ 251 764   UD 508 669
Causal Explanations of Male and Female Academic Performance as a Function of Sex-Role Biases. Post, Robin Dee. *Sex Roles: A Journal of Research*; v7 n7 p691–98 Jul 1981.
Descriptors: *Attribution Theory; Failure; Psychological Character-istics; *Sex Differences; Success.

Reports on a study designed to assess whether attributions of causality of success and failure would vary as a function of sex role attitudes. Indicates that sex-typed notions about competence may still be deeply ingrained despite recent social changes. (Author/MK)

EJ 251 765   UD 508 670
Sex Differences in Self-Concept and Self-Esteem of Late Adolescents: A Time-Lag Analysis. Lerner, Richard M.; And Others. *Sex Roles: A Journal of Research*; v7 n7 p709–22 Jul 1981
                                              (*CIJE*, 14 (1), 1982)

There is little doubt that the organization of the research literature has increased the efficiency of use, despite the cost of a tendency towards standardization and uniformity in the use of both language and ideas. However, in many applied studies the problem is not one of coming to terms with an existing research literature so much as coming to terms with an immediate research problem. Switching the focus from the research user to the research producer sometimes involves breaking the very assumptions that make large-scale retrieval systems possible. For while large-scale systems provide access they do so on the basis of a certain motivation and interest on the part of the user. Often in applied studies this cannot be assumed, for the heart of the problem may be one of communicating research to individuals or groups who do not share a research interest and who find the language of research off-putting. Generally, teachers, administrators and parents do not turn to abstracts when faced with a problem of a research kind; they tend to work within the constraints and possibilities of the situation at hand.

In discussing research techniques in the previous chapter, it became evident that to shift the audience for research to include those involved in the education process (other than researchers) has considerable implications for the process and presentation of research studies. In part this is a question of language – of finding non-technical and non-threatening ways to write about and talk about research studies and research findings. It means assuming a more active communicative (even a teaching) role, for the researcher cannot take for granted that the audience shares a common background understanding, a motivation and a set of interests and concerns that match his or her own. On the contrary, to include other audiences is to invite diverging perceptions, points of view and judgements into the process of research, and to make presentation a more central concern.

Consideration of alternative forms and formats of presentation may need to be made in the design stage of the study. Applied research may be most effectively communicated through oral presentations (to a school staff meeting, working group or committee), through the replay of audio-visual recordings (as part of a display for teachers, children and parents for instance), or in literary forms different from those of the research paper. While the use of these alternatives does not preclude the writing of conventional research reports, the latter may be seen as only one product of the research, and perhaps one of not too great a significance, depending on how important it is to communicate to academic audiences.

What is important is to start from the context of use, taking into account which audience you are attempting to reach, what media are most appropriately used and what forms of presentation are most likely to be effective. Identifying constraints and possibilities is important, as important as consideration of the academic content of the presentation. If you have only a ten-minute space in which to present your report it is little use talking fast and stopping when the time runs out. You have to decide what is the most effective use that can be made of ten minutes, or of sixty pages, or of a one-hour meeting or a two-hour in-service course.

Finding effective means of communication in applied research studies is an area that is undeveloped in relation to the effort that has gone into devising methods and techniques of data collection. Good examples are not easy to find, though in the rest of this chapter I will include a number of examples that may provide starting-points for further experimentation.

Robert Stake has for some years advocated the use of 'portrayal' (as opposed to analysis) in reporting evaluation studies. Stake argues that an evaluation cannot maintain a focus on both analysis and portrayal simultaneously: 'What the evaluator has to say cannot be both a sharp analysis of high-priority achievement *and* a broad and accurate reflection of the program's complex transactions. One message crowds out the other' (Stake, 1972, 1). The same point is generally true in research studies; the kind of investment of time and other resources necessary to complete a survey or testing programme, or to carry out a detailed ethnography, rarely leaves room for a full portrayal of the whole context within which the study was made. A choice has to be made between breadth and depth.

In an early attempt to provide such a 'portrayal', Stake and Gjerde, in an evaluation of a summer school programme in 'Twin City', produced a small pamphlet written in newspaper format. This attempted no analysis though it did include judgements made by students who elected to follow the options:

Ecological Biology

55 students
Masters: Tony Angellar, Harold Strobel; Assoc.: Bill Holmson

Aims. Through team teaching, to pose and ponder questions about the basic functions and reactions of animals and man, e.g., organismic learning, body-environment interaction, chronobiology. To measure and plot circadian rhythms, to carry on individual and group projects.

Sketch. Completed units on animal behavior, learning, body-environmental interaction, chronobiology, and circadian rhythm. Completed fewer projects than intended.

Comment. Great variety of field events; teacher-talk good talk, but probably too much of it.

Dance

35 students
Master: Mary Rae Josephson; Assoc.: Linda Nelson, Avi Davis

Aims. To involve each student in moving, thinking, feeling situations; encouraging student to rely on an expanding movement vocabulary, an awareness of self and sensitivity toward others, an increasing knowledge of dance as an art form and its relation to the other arts, a desire to express oneself creatively.

Sketch. Improvement of self-image and group awareness were seen as the two main accomplishments, with variation, of course, across individuals. Time spent in sustained warm-ups, body movement assignments, watching films of master dancers; in theme development, learning concentration, and developing a viable group.

Comment. Teachers highly competent, worked well together and with other teachers. Class needs boys, should be organized as supporting rather than as a principal enrollment.

Astronomy

32 students
Master: Fred Brett; Assoc.: Dennis Mallum

Aims. To examine the interdependence of scientific facts as they relate to events of the universe. To develop analytic and inferential skills. Individual projects, particularly building personal telescopes.

Sketch. Large blocks of time spent on grinding, polishing lenses. Used U. of Illinois Astronomy Series for background. Camped out to use their telescopes.

Comment. Students took great pride in their work. Sustained involvement.

Writers' Workshop

25 students
Master: Hu Anderson; Assoc.: R. Klepperich

Aims. To give students who want to learn to write a chance to learn about their writing. To learn how to search for things worth writing about.

Sketch. A subgroup of the class published 'La Bouche,' the student newspaper; others in class wrote stories and developed their personal writing styles.

Comment. A strange class, probably the least learning-oriented in the Institute. Students were not pushed to produce; many did not. More than half the students wished they had enrolled in something else – for the rest of the Institute only 15 per cent had that wish.

(Stake and Gjerde, 1974, 116–17)

Unlike conventional research reports this was written quickly (over a weekend, according to some of Stake's graduate students who worked on the project) and made available on a wide scale to those who took part in the programme.

A problem that arises with this kind of report is that of how to write the conclusions, summary or recommendations. Stake chose to include the following two statements, one from an advocacy position and one from an adversarial stance, and to present these side by side at the end of the report without further comment. (Since then more extensive procedures have been developed for handling what have become known as 'adversarial' evaluations – see, for example, Wolf, 1975, and Popham and Carlson, 1977.)

An Advocate's Statement

No visitor who took a long, hard look at TCITY-1971 kept his skepticism. A young visitor knows how precious it is to discover, to be heard, to belong. An older visitor knows the rarity of a classroom where teachers and students perceive each other as real people. To the nonvisitor it doesn't seem possible that a summer school program can deliver on all these promises to over 800 kids, but TCITY-1971 did.

Every curriculum specialist fears that by relaxing conduct rules and encouraging student independence they may be saying goodbye to the hard work and hard thinking that education requires. TCITY-1971 teachers and students made learning so attractive, so purposive, that free-ranging thought returned again and again to curricular themes: awareness of the human condition, obstacles to communications, ecological interactions, etc.

TCITY excels because of its staff. Its students give it movement. Its directors give it nurture. Its teachers give it movement, nurture, and direction. It would be incorrect to say that Mr. Caruson, Mr. Rose, and the teachers think alike as to the prime goals and methods of education, but collectively, they create a dynamic, humanistically bent, academically based curriculum.

The quality of teaching this summer was consistently high, from day to day, from class to class. Some of the teachers chose to be casual, to offer 'opportunities', to share a meaningful experience. Others were more intense, more intent upon sharing information and problem-solving methods. Both kinds were there, doing it well.

The quality of the learning also was high. The students were tuned in. They were busy. They responded to the moves of their teachers. They improvised; they carried ideas and arguments, indignations and admirations to the volleyball court, to the Commons, to the shade of campus elms and Cannon River oaks. The youngsters took a long step toward maturity.

True, it was a costly step. Thousands of hours, thousands of dollars, and at least a few hundred aggravations. But fit to a scale of public school budgets – and budgets for parks, interstate highways, and weapons of war – TCITY-1971 rates as a *best buy*. Eight hundred kids, give or take a few, took home a new talent, a new line of thinking, a new awareness – a good purchase.

It cannot be denied that other youngsters in Minneapolis and St. Paul deserve an experience like this. They should have it. Some say,

'TCITY is bad because it caters to the elite.' But a greater wisdom says 'Any effort fixated on giving an equal share of good things to all groups is destined to share nothing of value.' For less advantaged youth, a more equitable share of educational opportunities should be guaranteed. But even in times of economic recession, opportunities for the talented should be protected.

TCITY-1971 has succeeded. It is even a best buy. It satisfies a social obligation to specially educate some of those who will lead – in the arts, in business, in government, in life. The teachers of TCITY-1971 have blended a summer of caring, caprice, openness, and intellectual struggle to give potential leaders a summer of challenge.

Robert Stake[2]
Evaluation Specialist, CIRCE

An Adversary's Statement

TCITY is not a *scandalum magnatum*. But it is both less than it pretends to be and more than it wishes to be. There is enough evidence at least to question certain facets of the Institute – if not to return a true bill against it. Costly, enlarging, innovative, exemplary: these Institute attributes are worthy of critical examination.

How costly is this Institute? Dollar costs are sufficient to give each group of six students $1,000 to design and conduct their own summer experience. Over 100 Upward Bound students could be readied for their college careers at Macalester. About 25 expert curriculum specialists could be supported for half a year to design and develop new curricula for the high school.

What is the cost of removing 800 talented leaders from the local youth culture? What is the cost of widening the experience gap between Institute students and their parents, and their teachers in 'regular' high school, and their non-Institute friends? Not enough here to charge neo-Fascist elitism. Enough to warrant discussion.

The Institute abounds with self-named innovators and innovations, with alternatives to the business-as-usual education of high schoolers. Note that the Institute is not promoted as an exemplary alternative *to* schooling. It seeks to promote the development of alternative forms of education *for* schools. And it is failing to do even that job. What is TCITY doing to demonstrate that the TCITY style of life could be lived in schools as we know them? Where in the regular school is the staff so crucial to the life of the Institute? The money? The administrative leadership? Where are the opportunities for the teachers,

---

[2] Prepared by R. Stake, not to indicate his opinion of the Institute, but as a summary of the most positive claims that might reasonably be made.

principals, superintendents to come and live that life that they might come to share in the vision? And where are the parents? TCITY should be getting poor grades on affecting the regular school program.

There are other dimensions of TCITY that puzzle the non-believer:

1. How long can in-class 'rapping' continue and still qualify as educative self-exploration? Are there quality control procedures in effect during the summer program: For example, when one-third to one-half a class is absent from a scheduled meeting, should not that be seen as an educational crisis by the instructor?
2. What does TCITY do to help students realize that the Institute standards are necessarily high, that the regular school norms and expectations do not count, that a heretofore 'best' becomes just a 'so-so'? There are unnecessarily disheartened students in TCITY.
3. Is it unreasonable to expect that more than two of 22 teachers or associate teachers would have some clear idea or plan for utilizing TCITY approaches or curricula in their regular classroom next fall?
4. Few students – or faculty – understand the selection procedures employed to staff the teaching cadre and to fill the student corps. Why should it be a mystery?

The worst has been saved for last. This report concludes with an assertion: The absence of a crucial dimension in the instructional life of TCITY, that of constructive self-criticism, is a near fatal flaw. The observation and interview notes taken by the adversary evaluator over four days contains but five instances of students engaging in, or faculty helping students to become skillful in, or desirous of, the cultivation of self-criticism. The instances of missed opportunities were excessive in my judgment. Worse, when queried by the writer, faculty and students alike showed little enthusiasm for such fare. Is it too much to expect from Institute participants after but four weeks? Seven may be insufficient. The staff post mortem, 'Gleanings,' is a start – but it seems odd to start at the end.

The paucity of occurrence is less damning than the absence of manifest, widespread intent. Certain classes accounted for all the instances observed. They did not appear to be accidental. The intent was there. An Institute for talented high school youth cannot justifiably fail to feature individual and group self-criticism.

Terry Denny
Evaluation Specialist

(Stake and Gjerde, 1974, 135–8)

The posing of alternative perceptions, views and judgements is a device now used with some frequency in evaluation studies. While there are risks in polarizing judgement data, adversarial statements do provide a kind of objectivity, or at least neutrality, for the evaluator, however precarious such a stance may prove to be in practice. MacDonald and Stake (1974), taking a line from Tom Stoppard to the effect that 'dialogue is the most effective form for the writer who does not know his own mind', developed the adversarial format into a dialogue form in reporting to a government committee on the issues facing them in funding curriculum development in the field of computer-assisted learning. The committee was unhappy with the format and discussion was deflected away from the substantive issues towards the conduct of the evaluation – always a risk for those who adopt a creative approach to formats of presentation!

In this extract from the report, which was written very early in the programme, before many of the curriculum development projects were under way, the dialogue turns to the topic of the evaluation itself, arguing that there is some danger in the structure of the programme that the evaluation might be biased towards an advocacy view:

'What's your worry exactly?'

'Members of the Committee have private as well as public interests. They have political as well as educational concerns. Some members of the Committee are affiliated with agencies or institutions that are benefiting from, or could benefit from, support from the National Programme. There are conflict of interest problems built into that situation. I would certainly hope that these interests are made explicit and that the people concerned do not, in fact, take part in discussions where their interests are involved.'

'That's a bit purist isn't it? You want to exclude from the discussion those who have the most detailed knowledge. It's a bit like cutting off your nose to spite your face. Look here! Computerised learning is in its infancy in this country. If you're going to represent on your Committee those who know the field, you're bound to get these affiliations. Surely the Parliamentary model of declaring an interest before engaging in a debate would be sufficient? In any case, even if I conceded that you have a point, it only applies to a minority of the Committee.'

'That's not going to satisfy anybody. The National Programme is going to make some bad investments in institutions or agencies which are represented on the Committee. It also worries me that a non education industry, the British computer industry, has a lot at stake, so that pressures for positive findings, or at least non-disruptive findings, might occur. It seems to me that the chances of advocative bias are also increased by the extensiveness of internal evaluation activity. We will need to look very closely at the validity of positive evaluation findings.'

'Can the Programme itself provide validity checks that would satisfy you?'

'I think the best checks consist of covering a range of views, a range of data, about what is going on in the National Programme, paying particular attention to the critics, as I believe MacDonald is doing.'

'Do you mean you would pay more attention to reports that come from the independent evaluators than from the Directorate?'

'Not at all. The best understandings of CAL are likely to come from the Projects and from the Programme Directorate. What I will be looking for from MacDonald is corroboration, elaboration, bases for confidence in, or challenges to, what the participants have to say.'

(MacDonald and Stake, 1974, 11)

Recasting research data in dialogue of a Socratic form requires considerable effort in organizing material, in writing to ensure balance and readability. For the form to work well demands the discipline of a tight logic. In addition, if the dialogue is to be research-based then the issues have to be culled from interview and other material, a process that can be extra-ordinarily time-consuming. MacDonald and Stake claim that most of what they included in their report was virtually transcribed from actual conversations and interviews, but closely edited and organized. It would have been simpler and more straightforward simply to list issues, and indeed the committee said they would have preferred this (a request that the evaluators did respond to eventually). However, although the dialogue and the issues list might seem merely alternative ways of presenting the same information, the story is not quite so simple. The very form of the dialogue makes a point not made in other ways. It invites participation; in itself it rejects (at one level) an authoritative judgement; it demonstrates 'open-endedness', divergence of view, unresolved conflict and discrepancy in a manner that statements cannot.

There are other ways dialogue might be used as a form of reporting. In producing a radio programme for the Open University, Pick and Walker (1976) used interview transcripts as the basis for producing a radio play. The theme was that of the role of the teacher in the process of curriculum development. The interviews were with science teachers who had been involved one way or another in curriculum development, and asked particularly about motivation, requiring the teachers to recount particular experiences. The mass of transcript material was handed to a playwright, who cut and edited it in order to create a 'play' which used the words spoken by some twenty teachers but organized them around four characters, whose comments were slotted into a narration which was edited from a diary one of the teachers had written:

(Fade up school and playground and hold under)

14. MELVYN BLOOM: The Head of Physics makes me insecure. He's a very nasty person, calls me 'bloody Smith'. I call him 'bloody Jones'. All good-humoured, but he definitely dislikes me and what I stand for. He's two years off retirement, and has taught here ever since the war, when he got the job after two hundred others had applied for it. Then he saw himself at the top of the scale, his pay on par with the local doctor. All this has vanished . . . he's not a happy man, and it's all *my* fault!

15. BARBARA GREEN: Life really is difficult in this school. One week I asked leave to attend a job interview, the headmaster advised me to give up teaching, *and* I was hit over the head by a pupil with a chair. Perhaps it's my problem, a problem I have to live with, which I can't unload. But a greater sense of belonging to a department would help. At least I'd get advice then and share it with others.
(School background into bell)

16. NARRATOR: 11.45 Lower Sixth. Most finishing notes as instructed. Go through filter action of *Glomerulus* and then set homework.
(Fade up school and playground)

17. SUSAN DALE: I think too much is expected of us. For most people it's impossible to do the job even adequately. People compensate; they compromise in the way that they teach, in the materials they prepare. The roles they're expected to play

are too wide and there are too many different ones. They're expected to be authoritarian and to relate to children at the same time. You've got to tell them off for not wearing school uniform and have a trusting relationship with them.

18. RICHARD CRANE: When the kids actually ask questions that I've not thought that they could, and when one of them goes further and expands something, and then the bell goes and they say 'that's not the bell, is it sir?' it's exhilarating. Mind you, it also makes me hopping mad. The bell controls their lives. Normally they pack up five minutes before it goes.
(School background into bell)

19. NARRATOR: 12.30 Lunch: Chat to two groups about 'open careers meeting' in library – a follow-on from last term. They decide to have it on Thursdays. Send note to careers master for OK. Another note back – 'yes – damn you'.

1.30 Back to lab. for own third form. Prepare demonstration of injected kidney.
(Bell)   (Pick and Walker, 1976, 14–15)

One of the features of this form of reporting is a massive process of selection in getting from the data available to the finished report. It is not simply a case, as in statistical processing, of condensing large amounts of information into more generalized and compressed statements, but of rejecting large quantities of information and making more of some of it than of the rest. In this sense decisions are made on the basis of judgements as to what is significant and what is trivial. In producing the radio play some of these judgements were of a technical or aesthetic kind; that is to say it meant looking not just at the point being made, but at how it was made. Some statements simply read well, involved graphic illustration or fitted well into the script at certain points. If you choose to work in a medium of this kind you cannot simply ignore the constraints that the medium itself imposes but have to make use of them; and as in any medium the conventions are likely to be controversial and problematic, so you have to be prepared to enter to some degree into the world of which they are a part, perhaps with the consequence that some research principles become compromised in the face of principles emanating from other sources.

The forces of compression are perhaps strongest in producing diagrams, charts or book covers. In research the temptation is always towards caution and elaboration, not qualities that catch the eye of a disinterested passing audience. To take on the role of advertiser and promoter runs counter to most of the basic values of research. On the other hand, there may be some things we can learn from other, very different, attempts to communicate. It was with this in mind that Barry MacDonald tried to compress all he had learnt in five years as evaluator of the Humanities Curriculum Project into a six-page fold-out pamphlet. In advertising and promotional terms this pamphlet was still loaded down with information and confused by cross-cutting multiple messages, but in academic terms it represented a novel attempt to compress what would have normally filled a book into a form where it could be circulated on a large scale and made available to large numbers of people.

Other experiments with presentation that are worthy of note here are: EPIE's summary of alternative early childhood intervention programmes produced on tape-slide (EPIE Information Unit, 1972); an attempt to evaluate an outward-bound programme using a combination of time series statistical analysis and a diary written by a participant (Smith, 1975); an attempt to produce a collage of quotes on the theme of the 'Nuffield Approach' (to science teaching) which took as its underlying model a musical score (Walker, 1974); a musical score (Mitchell, in Fox, 1978); and photographic records (Fox *et al.*, 1975).

It has to be said that these, and most other, attempts to experiment with different forms of presentation have generally failed to reach other audiences on a wide scale, though they have often irritated and even angered academics, research sponsors and decision-makers. Those who find this an area of applied research in need of development and critical attention (and I include myself) have to face the fact that while it can be a rewarding area in which to work, it is not one that can be taken for granted. Innovations in presentational format have to be made with some care to the process of explaining and justifying the approaches used to those most affected by them. It is an area where little can be taken for granted or on trust.

In this chapter I have stressed possible alternative forms for

SAFARI PROFILES

INSTRUCTION IN OBEDIENCE?
aim J to the un- self om-

Row over race pack

Can't teachers be trusted any more?

HCP – A QUIET EDUCATIONAL REVOLUTION

Thumbnail Social History of Humanities Curriculum Project

The team saw themselves as a 'research' group offering schools new knowledge and hypotheses about enquiry teaching, rather than prescribing a curriculum. "We have nothing to recommend", said Stenhouse. But teacher 'neutrality' was a provocative concept, and they were soon caught up in an inflationary spiral of rhetorical debate, at its most public when their collection of materials on Race was suppressed by Schools Council in a blaze of publicity. Condemned by NUT and NAS spokesmen, cut adrift by Council (though not by Nuffield), and assailed variously from the Left — "bourgeois indoctrination", from the Right — "dangerous revolution", by academics — "ethical relativism", and by activists — "substituting social action with a parlour game", the project was vigorously defended by an equally diverse range of allies, and acquired something of a 'cult' reputation while continuing to compete successfully in the market place. A recent survey of project adoption by the Chelsea Centre for Science Education has placed HCP ahead of the field.

Although HCP was by no means an 'auteur project' (the team was large and unusually powerful), Stenhouse was a strong leader and remains an enigmatic figure. To admirers, the most imaginative curriculum developer of them all ("a chess player in a world of draughts",) to detractors an over-intellectual entrepreneur. Welcomed with open jaws by the philosophers of education (he engaged in their discourse and invited curriculum analysis), disliked by the policy-makers (he wouldn't simplify and cultivated paradox), he is, unlike most project directors, still active in the curriculum research field.

A One Sentence Description

A five-year research, development, evaluation and dissemination programme concerned with the discussion by adolescent pupils of controversial social and moral issues.

Time Scale

1967-70 (the initial period of funding by Schools Council and Nuffield)
1970-72 (the extension, by Schools Council, mainly for further evaluation and dissemination)

The Location

1967-70 Philippa Fawcett College, London
1970-72 Centre for Applied Research in Education (CARE), University of East Anglia
(initiative by Schools Council out of its growing concern for continuity and aftercare)

Published Collections (by Heinemann Educational Books)

	Sales (to January 1975)
The Family (1970)	1442
War and Society (1970)	1238
Education (1970)	976
Relations Between the Sexes (1970)	898
People and Work (1971)	894
Poverty (1971)	606
Law and Order (1972)	570
Living in Cities (1973)	465

Complete packs £36 + VAT

Main Project Team	Came From	Stayed	Responsible For	Went To
Lawrence Stenhouse	College of Ed.	from 1967	Rel. bet. Sexes	University (CARE)
Gillian Box	Careers Centre	67-70	Production	Schools Council
John Elliott	School	from 1967	War/People & Work	University (CARE)
Maurice Plaskow	BBC	67-70	Family	Schools Council
Jean Rudduck	College of Ed.	from 1967	Dissemination	University (CARE)
John Hipkin	Research Unit	68-70	Education/Race	Schools Council
Pat Haikin	College of FE	68-70	Poverty	College of FE
Jim Hillier	College of FE	68-69	Film Research	BFI

(Also involved for shorter periods were: A. Cook, D. Vignali, A. McTaggart, R. Bland, A. Dale).

Cost

Approximately £250000 (including evaluation)

Development Trials

1968-70 36 schools from 29 Local Educational Authorities in England and Wales. Urban and rural schools, secondary modern and comprehensives.

Background to the Project

1. **Raising of the School Leaving Age** (expected in 1970, implemented in 1972).
2. **Newsome Report** (1963)   HCP team did not like its acceptance of a special curriculum for the non-academic and rarely quoted it.

3. **Working Paper No. 11**   (Schools Council 1967). This was the Feasibility Study for HCP, but they did not like it either, and only used it to support the idea of 'areas of enquiry'.
4. **Working Paper No. 2**   (Schools Council 1965). This paper, with its high aspirations for 'everyman', its assertion that the limitations of the pupil had to be identified and not assumed, and its emphasis on the pursuit of understanding, came closest to the values of the team and was liberally quoted by them.

Interpreting the Remit

The team defined humanities as "the study of important human issues", the aim of the project as "to develop an understanding of human acts, of social situations, and of the problems of value which arise from them" and the curriculum problem as "how is a teacher in a democracy to handle controversial value issues?"

Premises

The work of the project was based upon five major premises:
1. that controversial issues should be handled in the classroom with adolescents.
2. that the teacher accepts the need to submit his teaching in controversial areas to the criterion of **neutrality** at this stage of education i.e. that he regards it as part of his responsibility not to promote his own view.
3. that the mode of enquiry in controversial areas should have discussion, rather than instruction, as its core.
4. that the discussion should protect divergence of view among participants, rather than attempt to achieve consensus.
5. that the teacher as chairman of the discussion should have responsibility for quality and standards in learning.

Strategy

a) Materials: Nine themes were chosen as areas of enquiry for experimental development. The team produced multi-media collections of study materials and teacher guides in each theme area and in cooperation with the British Film Institute a film-hire service.

b) Pedagogy: Basically enquiry through classroom discussion, with the teacher, in the role of 'neutral chairman', attempting to promote reflective interpretation of 'evidence' drawn from the theme collections.

Dissemination

Aim. "to establish by 1972 sufficient people throughout the country with understanding and energy enough to ensure that the experiment could be sustained, that new people could be

Poverty

effectively brought in, that experience could be shared and learned from and that standards could be effectively re-thought."

Main Strategy: Training through centrally-held courses, teams of people from LEAs who then (at least theoretically) take responsibility locally for teacher training and support. Such courses, initiated in 1970, are still going on under the aegis of CARE, which maintains contact with a network of local contacts throughout the country.

The project's ideas and principles are difficult to grasp or have been poorly communicated, or both. **Exception** — the central courses which seem very effective and produce understanding and enthusiasm.

A Guide to the Observer of HCP

1. At the LEA level.

HCP can be a risky enterprise for the teacher, both in career and political terms. Legitimation and informed external support are therefore important, especially when not provided by the school. Some LEAs will back teachers who fear adverse community reaction, others firmly decline.

Training provision for new HCP teachers essential.

Hire of films for use in HCP schools often depends on financial support from LEA.

2. At the school level.

Time allocation less important than viable group size, physical conditions (private and quiet) and access to materials (storage and retrieval are problems). Support of headmaster more important than that of colleagues. Danger of project being perceived as "softsell" if confined to low status pupils and teachers. In schools with exam emphasis, some teachers say HCP must be examined to gain commitment of staff and pupils. Others disagree, some hotly. Project Team stayed neutral on this issue.

3. **At the classroom level.**

Organisation: HCP discussion difficult to realise with groups of more than 15-mixed ability best, but not 'ad hoc' mixtures. Circular seating but semi-formal (i.e. with desks) best bet. Single sex groups disadvantaged with most themes. Experienced teachers more likely to succeed, even though more ingrained in previous practice.

Teacher Role Characteristics: does not express views, listens, summarises, controls interruptions, introduces new evidence, encourages pupils to concentrate on interpreting the materials, forestalls premature or social consensus on issues, tolerates silence, invites comment on his role performance.

Pupil Role Characteristics: addresses group rather than teacher, listens to views of others, refrains from personalised criticism, calls for new evidence, takes responsibility for maintaining the enquiry and for new initiatives.

Additional Note.

Adversaries of HCP are critical of the difficulty level of the materials: advocates respond that the HCP discussion process enables pupils to tackle successfully as a group materials they could not cope with as individuals. Adversaries claim that pupils must be able to understand the material *before* they can discuss it: advocates claim that understanding is the *product* not the *prerequisite* of discussion — "You discuss because you do not understand".

The process of conventional discussion		The HCP process	
1. READ	(pupils read the material)	1. READ	(pupils read the materials)
2. UNDERSTAND	(teacher tests individual comprehension)	2. DISCUSS	(pupils help each other interpret the materials)
3. DISCUSS	(pupils exchange opinions)	3. UNDERSTAND	(pupils explore their differing interpretations and reactions to the materials)

HCP EVALUATION

Time Scale: 1968-70 Philippa Fawcett College, London.
1970-73 CARE, University of East Anglia

Personnel: 1968-73 Barry MacDonald (now SAFARI director)
1970-72 G K Verma, S Humble, H Simons

Design Combination of clinical, psychometric and sociometric studies.

Phase One (1968-70) Formative evaluation for central team, narrative chronicle of Project history, case studies of trial schools.

Phase Two (1970-73) Measurement of pupil change, case studies of schools and LEAs, surveys of adoption, studies of dissemination. Extensive publication, mainly to participants, during this period.

Results

Case Study HCP difficult to assimilate — schools much more authoritarian than they realise — HCP creates dissonance at all levels of impact: persistence needed to achieve satisfaction and stability of process. Institutional context important but unpredictable. Individual pupil, teacher and school reactions range from dismal failure to spectacular success.

Measurement Test programme over-ambitious and seriously flawed in execution — nevertheless suggests that in the hands of trained teachers pupils gain in language skills and self-esteem.

Survey Adoption comparatively widespread — mainly by English and History teachers in mid-career — FAMILY and WAR the favourite topics.

OVERVIEW OF PROJECT IMPACT

Considerable impact on professional debate about the role of the teacher and the responsibility of schools for moral education — some impact on curriculum and innovation theory — national impact on school practice largely unknown although commercially successful. The persistence of interest in HCP may be a testimony to the importance of the problem or the remedy — or both.

The HCP 'Race' Experiment

A cautious approach confined to six schools, designed primarily to test Miller's conclusion that teaching about race per se increases prejudice. Heavily evaluated, results did not confirm Miller. Schools and team wanted to go on, but were blocked by the Schools Council after consultations with the Race Relations Board, who were hostile to the project. Eventually, the SSRC sponsored further work in Race by the HCP team. This work will continue to 1977.

HCP in Approved Schools

Although a 'progressive elite' of four schools successfully took part in the trial phase, (negotiated by the Home Office soon after the Court Lees scandal), subsequent dissemination efforts were ineptly coordinated and abortive.

The Catholic Schools Sub-Project

Set up by the Catholic Education Board after Stenhouse "converted" Derek Morell (Schools Council, joint author of Working Paper 2) it was run from Strawberry Hill College by Tony Higgins (see 'Towards Judgement' for details). Some Catholic schools saw no need for a separate project. The Sub-Project reinterpreted 'neutrality' theory theologically in terms of "primacy of conscience" and tried to produce materials which strengthened Catholic sources across the range of themes. Materials not approved by the Board for publication.

The Project Abroad

HCP has attracted its share of interest, particularly in USA, Canada, Australia, New Zealand, Scandinavia, West Germany, Ireland and Scotland. Reactions worth noting:

USA — apparent conflict with educational drive for social consensus through values curriculum.
West Germany — big impact on national debate about 'open curricula'. Criticised by radical reformists as 'bourgeois'.
N. Ireland – toyed with as a possible instrument of reconciliation, but too 'risky'.

Eire —Materials and method embodied in Dublin Vocational Schools Humanities Project.

Implementation in other countries inhibited by the need to regenerate the materials, which are not only language-bound but culture-bound too.

SOURCES OF FURTHER INFORMATION

Centre for Applied Research in Education, University of East Anglia. Available books, "Towards Judgement" and "People in Classrooms". Further volumes anticipated.

SAFARI is a follow-up study of four completed curriculum projects. Information about SAFARI, and profiles of Project Technology, Geography for the Young School Leaver, and Nuffield Secondary Science, are obtainable from the Centre for Applied Research in Education, University of East Anglia, NR2 7JT. SAFARI staff: B. MacDonald, R. Walker.

written reports; some discussion of the forms available for presenting visual material will be found in Chapter 4.

In summarizing, it is necessary to point out that there has generally been a good deal more experimentation with research techniques than there has been with presentational forms. Alternative forms of presentation are perhaps by their nature more difficult to find and to document, but they also challenge more fundamental assumptions than those raised by innovations at the technical level. To change the form of presentation is to raise questions about reporting research to other audiences. It is a fundamental belief in science, and one which has been carried over into social science and into educational research, that research is primarily reported to the scientific peer group. It is this 'invisible college' which scrutinizes research, and through a process of critical debate and a 'free market' mechanism of acknowledgment and reference, admits it to the status of received knowledge.

To suggest that research might, or ought, to report primarily to other audiences, and particularly to professional and lay audiences who have legitimate rights and vested interests, is to challenge values basic to the scientific enterprise. While there might seem to be good reasons for closing the gap between research and practice from the professional viewpoint, such values serve to maintain independence, objectivity and credibility in research and should not be transgressed lightly. To write research studies for audiences other than for the invisible college might seem, from a professional point of view, self-evidently a good thing to do, but it should be realized that to attempt to do so is to enter long-standing and fiercely defended positions in the history and philosophy of science.

6 Developing a community of knowledgeable users

In concluding this book I want to return to some of the themes first raised in Chapter 1, where I indicated that what was distinctive about applied research was the relationship it implied between those who do research, those who are subject to research, and those who make use of research.

In conventional research designs the relationship between those who do research and those who are subjects of study is primarily a question of minimizing interference effects in order to maximize objectivity, a process that may need to be set against the need to consider the rights of those involved. This has become an increasingly important consideration in the social and human sciences, particularly in the USA, where the threat of legal action has led many institutions to establish 'Research on Human Subjects' committees, which vet prospective research and may withhold approval if the legal risk looks high.

I have argued here for an interactive relationship between researcher and subjects, not out of legal considerations but in order to increase the responsiveness of the researcher to the problems, issues and work conditions of the subject. The argument for interaction has been that, in applied studies, the need to fit the design and practice of research to the needs and conditions of the subject overrides the requirements of objectivity necessary in studies that aim for precise statements of a generalized kind.

Applied studies of the kind described and advocated in this book remain close to specifics and are context bound. They rarely claim generalized results, though they may imply consequences for circumstances beyond the particular site studied.

They provide a basis for generalizing *to* other circumstances and situations, but do not make generalizations *from* particular studies to statements of a theoretical kind. A similar situation exists in some branches of engineering. Research done in order to build a suspension bridge draws on theoretical statements of a general kind as background, but the studies that are made add little to the world of theory. They do, however, make building the bridge possible. As successive bridges are constructed a body of applied research emerges which makes the building of larger and more efficient designs feasible. The underlying physics of such bridges is the same, but the applied knowledge needed to build them did not previously exist. It could only be won by experience. (Tom Fox has pointed out to me that the same is true of aeroplane design: knowing the theory is insufficient to produce a design for a 747.)

In education, applied research should be used in similar ways. It should be interactive with experience and practice, seeking to extend the scope and application of innovation, to increase efficiency, and to concentrate its attention on the relation between design and performance. This is clearly not to argue for applied research as an alternative to pure, or conventional, research. There is a necessary relationship between applied and scientific research: both should be dependent on each other. It is, however, to argue for the emergence of an applied tradition that has been slow to emerge in the human and social sciences. For while the labels of application abound (particularly in psychology), the press for (and dependence on) theory has been too strong. Research designs have overemphasized objectivity at the cost of responsiveness and attention to context, and social theory has kept a social distance.

Some will object to the insistent use of the term 'applied' to preface 'educational research'. They will argue that educational research is inevitably applied and to use the term at all is to concede an advantaged position to conventional (social science) research in education. I would accept the point, but in practice I find that to omit the word 'applied' makes the text less clear. Using it serves as a constant reminder.

Applied research also means rethinking the relationship between the research and the user. The standard model in research is one that sees research being disseminated in a free market. Given access to publication, which is constrained by economic factors but controlled by academic peers, research finds its way to its users on merit and utility. When this proves too weak a delivery system it may be enhanced by the setting of special conferences and promotional campaigns or by the media. (Consider, for example, the ways in which research on the effects of smoking has been disseminated.)

In all these dissemination models the assumption remains of an essentially consumer market. Some people do research; others use it: and questions of method are, for the most part, technical questions concerning only the producers.

The kind of applied research I have been writing about in this book draws on different assumptions. It tends to be small scale, even amateur, but it attempts to involve the consumer in questions of process and method to the extent that what becomes disseminated is not 'findings' but a research approach. Rather than influence consumer attitudes by careful use of hard facts (as anti-smoking campaigns attempt to do), applied research attempts to provide the consumer with test instruments, or at least with a set of attitudes which allows them to collect and assess information about themselves in particular social contexts.

As I have argued previously, this is not to frame an alternative that excludes conventional research, but is rather to open up ways of thinking about (and doing, and using) research that add another dimension to the enterprise. Such a conception of research requires certain conditions and circumstances in which to become established and to survive. Susan Cosgrove, a teacher in Australia, has described these conditions as follows:

1. the willingness of teachers to critically examine their practice;
2. the willingness to communicate their findings to other teachers to make public what happens in their classrooms and why it happens that way;
3. the willingness to involve the students in the action research process, by negotiating with them about the procedure, consulting them regularly and sharing the information collected with them. The students are therefore participants in the critical community;
4. the existence of people who can give moral support during the process. In our system, some of these people have to be in authority positions in the hierarchical structure;

5. the willingness of the teacher to articulate the theory which her practice describes; and
6. the development of an understanding of, and an ability to manage, the politics of action research, that is, the ability to cope with, and counter, the inevitable criticism that comes from colleagues, students and parents.

(Cosgrove, 1981, 21)

But these are not simply preordinate and necessary conditions, they are conditions that may in turn be fostered and encouraged by research. Read through the other end of the telescope these same conditions might function as a list of aims and outcomes for applied research. And it is important to note that they are aims and outcomes that are primarily educational in character, so while applied research in management, or in occupations, or in medicine, might share characteristics with applied research in education, our field remains distinguished by educational intent. Unlike much conventional educational research, which finds justification for itself in the assumptions of the social sciences, applied research in education self-consciously sets out to improve educational practice.

I pause, because that phrase is sure to curl the edges of any reader coming from a social science background, where the first lesson one is taught is that the role of social scientist is positive rather than normative. The research task, in conventional terms, is to describe, not to prescribe. Yet we know this is not the case. Even in education some of the best research has served to grind sharp axes. The theme of inequality of educational opportunity in the sociology of education, for instance, can scarcely claim to have been conducted out of political disinterest. Nevertheless, the myth has persisted that we can be objective in our methods and in our findings and reserve bias for interpretation (a part of the process that can be kept until the last page of the report).

To put improvement in education at the front of the enterprise is to break a fundamental rule because it is seen to weaken the very structure of the research enterprise. How can we expect those who argue against reform to take us seriously if we admit our bias from the start?

There is of course some truth in this charge, though whether or not we admit bias is perhaps not relevant in practice, as we will no doubt be assumed to be biased however much we profess disinterest.

From the point of view of applied research prior commitment is necessary in order to secure access and to define an educational role for the project. There are few who would deny that educational improvement is a worthwhile aim; where they are certain to differ is in defining objectives. The battleground of applied research usually proves to lie in competing for the ground to define improvement, and that results in a series of hand-to-hand encounters which are of a different character to the long-range artillery typically exchanged over issues such as educational selection and access to opportunity in relation to social class. From the outside it may well appear compromised and accepting of existing structures. From the inside it may be justified as the long march through the institutions.

Bev Beasley and Lorraine Riordan have spelt out in a little more detail how the relationship between educational research and teacher research might be recast more productively:

We felt that the gulf between research bodies and the teaching profession has ensured that many research programmes are not related to the concerns and interests of teachers and students. Priorities for research too often reflect the interests of academic researchers or central office administrators not school people. Teachers and students in the classroom are rarely actively engaged in the research. Within the experimental framework the researcher protects his or her independence for the sake of 'objectivity'. The tacit knowledge of teachers is devalued. Many of the findings are recorded in a form and style which is accessible to the trained researcher but fails to communicate to teachers, school administrators, parents or advisory people. The primary audience for research has been the research community *not* the practising teacher. Not surprisingly we the practising teachers have come to distrust and reject theoretical research and the researcher who takes but does not give.

The Teacher and Research (Brian Cane and Colin Schroeder, 1970) contains many examples of how teachers feel about the researcher's inability to understand their situation. 'What do they know about teaching? They don't come in and face thirty-six children every morning' (p. 40). After such research has been collated and, if the school is fortunate enough to receive the results, is there a likelihood that the research outcomes will influence classroom practice? Cane and Schoeder's findings, based on what teachers told them, make this seem unlikely. 'Teachers felt that reading research was a small part of their professional life.' Research writings '. . . were often incomprehensible, too long, phrased in tactless language, biased in their presentation or of limited applicability.' However teachers ' . . . were enthusiastic about research publications that spoke directly to the classroom teacher'. (p. 60)

Our working group was concerned to shift the locus of control of curriculum research to the classroom teacher. We reasoned that research initiated and carried out by the teachers in their classrooms had great potential to affect classroom practice because it could:

- begin with, and build on, the knowledge teachers had already accumulated through experience
- focus on the immediate interests and concerns of classroom teachers
- better match the subtle organic processes of classroom life
- build on the 'natural' processes of evaluation and research which teachers carry out daily
- bridge the gap between understanding and action by merging the role of the researcher and practitioner.

Teachers who actively participated in the research enterprise would be more committed to act on the findings and develop their *own* options for change.

Research carried out by teachers in classrooms could:

- sharpen teachers' critical awareness through observation, recording and analysis of classroom events. It could be a consciousness-raising exercise.
- provide teachers with better information than they already have about what is actually happening in the classroom and why.
- help teachers better articulate teaching and learning processes to their colleagues and interested community members.
- bridge the gap between theoretic research and practice-based research. Teacher-researchers, Don Graves said, 'become consumers and critics of research literature'.

(Beasley and Riordan, 1981, 36)

It might be thought that to develop teacher research requires radically rethinking what might be thought to be the basic skills of research, and particularly writing skills. Given the blueprint that Beasley and Riordan sketch out it would seem at first sight that alternative communication and dissemination systems are called for. The classical device of publication through journals is perhaps inappropriate when the emphasis of the work is on groups and networks actively collaborating in the research. In this context the main outcomes of research are likely to be discussion documents, discussion itself and a plethora of multimedia, multi-channel, mostly locally disseminated materials. The parallel is perhaps of cable television as compared to state-owned national networks, or of community presses as compared to national daily newspapers.

It is possible to detect something of this trend. Areas that have developed strong applied research traditions have produced a kind of underground press, some of which has found its way into this book. On the other hand the normal mechanism of research dissemination through an invisible, academically orientated college has always played a major role. Documents such as the Ford Teaching Project booklets, while they might have been written primarily for other teachers, have tended only to reach other teachers through networks which involve academics in dominant roles. Perhaps there are no dangers in this and perhaps it is a natural system to make use of in promoting ideas. On the other hand there are those who argue that there is an inevitable back-wash effect – that if academics occupy gate-keeping positions then their interests, values and criteria will come to dominate the directions in which developments take place (for example, Nixon (1981) makes this point). Certainly it seems true that a major factor in promoting the idea of applied or action research has been the openness of award-bearing courses to curriculum changes of this kind, especially in the in-service area – a factor that in itself has brought academics into a position of prominence.

In part this is perhaps why the traditional research skills have lingered longer than might be expected. People do still write in forms and styles that are relatively conventional, certainly conventional enough to find their way into standard publications, even though the logic of the situation might seem to be one that would lead to an emphasis on oral and visual forms of reporting, and to forms of presentation that diverge considerably from standard publication.

The continuing emphasis on literary forms of presentation, and on forms that do not stray far from academic conventions, may be explained in part by the continued dominance of award-bearing courses. Many of those papers that publish results of action research and applied research were written, in part at least, as essays, assignments and dissertations for course-work assessment. On the other hand, there are those who have argued that the process of writing is itself at the heart of the research process. Stephen Rowland, for instance, working with a group of teachers observing and researching in classrooms and looking particularly at children's own work, has emphasized that through writing children often come to understandings that they would not have otherwise reached (Rowland, 1981, 1982; see also Armstrong, 1981). The same process applies to teachers, a point also made by Bev Beasley in a paper that builds on the article quoted earlier:

When there is a collection of your own and others' narratives it becomes more possible to see emerging shapes. The process of clarifying and ordering can become more precise.

- Are there common elements which re-occur?
- Is there a sequence of events?
- Are there patterns of elements?
- Are there significant issues?
- How are these things related to one another?

What is recognised can then be questioned.

- Why did I notice (observe) these particular things? What is influencing my noticing?
- Why can I so easily fit these elements together into a comfortable pattern?
- Why are there these contradictions? Where do they come from?

These are not all the possible questions arising from shaping but these kinds of questions can begin to bring to consciousness some of the assumptions that are implicit in practices. There is also opportunity to explore their origins and effects. In doing this the individual begins moving into the social sphere. Henry Giroux, when discussing a possible new sociology of curriculum in education, wrote:

The new mode of curriculum must be deeply personal. But only in the sense that it recognises individual uniqueness and needs *as a part of a specific social reality*. Individual and social needs have to be linked and mediated through a critical perspective tied to notions of emancipation. (1981, 253)

When there is an accumulation of writing and talking from all those involved, this kind of questioning allows a critical examination that is firmly grounded in social context. The questions: What have we learned? and What do we want to change? begin to take on a wider perspective.

(Beasley, 1981, 50)

The implication here is for a process role for writing; writing becomes an extension of, or a tool of, thought as well as a vehicle for carrying information. Conflict with conventional research models can arise, for in many areas of research the conventions of scientific reporting have been adopted. These conventions reduce the subjective content of reports to a minimum and tend to report research in a cryptic fashion that invokes a code understood only by those actively involved in the same field. The separation between reporting findings and speculation has closed in the field of applied or action research, and the two tend to be presented as closely related. Thus the advice given by Nisbet and Entwhistle (1970), while much of it is sound, may seem inappropriate in the context of applied or action research, where the aim is not to 'convey information to other scholars' but to reach other audiences directly. The standard framework

1. An outline of the research.
2. A review of previous work.
3. A precise statement of the scope and aims of the investigation.
4. Description of the procedure, the sample and the test measurements used.
5. Statement of results.
6. Discussion.
7. Summary and conclusions.
8. List of references.

(Nisbet and Entwhistle, 1970, 168)

may be useful to bear in mind, but it may not be the best framework to apply to the writing of a document for a staff meeting, a report written for parents or children to read, or a summary statement of issues arising from a curriculum analysis, an evaluation of a course, or a report on an in-service course.

Nisbet and Entwhistle's general advice on clichés ('dodges') remains as important as ever. Clarity, brevity and force of argument are enduring virtues worth striving for, and every word processor should be programmed to reject the following:

'The results obtained from three of the subjects were selected for detailed study.' (Translation: 'The results of the others didn't make sense and were therefore ignored'.)

'Previous research has shown that . . .' ('I couldn't be bothered to look up the references.')

'Results indicate that. . . .' ('I can't prove it, but this is what I believe.')

'Results suggest that . . . .' ('The results were not significant.')

'It is obvious that, well known that, generally accepted that. . . .' ('No evidence available.')

'This aspect requires further research.' ('I can't make head nor tail of it myself.')

'. . . . a pilot study . . . .' ('No significant results, but my promotion is coming up shortly.')

'A content analysis of forty-three items in the inventory identified eight distinguishable categories.' ('I looked at the cards and put them into eight piles.')

'Full details of the statistical procedure will be found in Guilford's *Psychometric Methods*.' ('I couldn't understand it myself.')

'A representative sample of university students.' ('My tutorial group.')

'Because of various complicating factors this group was omitted from the analysis.' ('I couldn't sort out the mess and scrapped the lot.')

(Nisbet and Entwhistle, 1970, 175)

What needs to be added to the quest for brevity, clarity and force of argument in applied and action research is a finely developed sense of audience and an ability to capture and develop interest in issues previously taken for granted. This is a need that invokes skills usually thought to be in the hands of journalists not academics, but it puts increased demands on the writer that cannot be neglected. To report only to other scholars is, in most cases, to fail.

Those who have been involved in action research and applied research in their own schools are aware of another dimension to the process which is political rather than academic. What are the implications for the school when one or more teachers begin organizing action research within the school? This question was addressed by the Classroom Action Research Network in its fourth annual conference in 1982 under the title 'Action Research into Action Research'. The report on the conference includes long lists of constraints and institutional interference effects, but also suggests some strategies for dealing with them.

The constraints include:

1. Decision-making structures.
2. Lack of time.
3. Isolation of teacher/researcher.
4. Standard criteria validating what counts as research.
5. Lack of recognition of need for research.
6. Lack of confidence by researcher.
7. Personality clashes.
8. Suspicion of new activities.
9. Different aims and objectives of colleagues.
10. Difficulties in communication.
11. Barriers of staff hierarchy (both ways).
12. Attitude of headteacher.
13. Lack of clarity about purposes and feasibility
14. Fear of probable unknowns of research.
15. Lack of knowledge of research methods.
16. Threat to autonomy of teachers.
17. Low morale.
18. Fear of criticism.
19. Getting parents to make a real contribution.
20. Lack of understanding of purpose of research.
21. Teacher/researcher seen as threat by staff.
22. Mixed abilities and mixed commitment of teachers.
23. Involving students.
24. Admitting to negative results to others.
25. Use of jargon.
26. Association with progressive (lefty) education.
27. Access to resources and facilities.
28. Difficulty of negotiating dissemination.
29. Problems of confidentiality.
30. Coping with directions: breadth vs. depth.
31. Lack of will to make decisions and take action.
32. Fear of tarnishing school image.
33. Political use/abuse by insiders/outsiders.
34. Poor communication within school.
35. Lack of familiarity and understanding by senior management.
36. Lack of participatory decision-making in school.
37. How do we know what is really happening in our research?
38. The ethics of involving students.
39. Keeping head above water once pushed off.

Suggested strategies include:

Suggested strategies for the lack of time constraint

adapt standard methods
be flexible
convince authority of need for more resources
clarification of task in small group/team discussion before whole staff
   work together
check on present use of time
timetable for research and support activities
try to delegate some of your responsibilities
use resources of students, university, college, etc.
a proper meeting calendar
use parents
learn to manage with less sleep
term in which research undertaken – autumn most favourable
management team undertake structured servicing of research,
   implementing action etc.
close school early one day a term
second staff
release staff using INSET money
be judicious in collecting data
seek co-operation of colleagues
team teaching
be nice to the office/clerical staff
don't transcribe everything
reappraisal of professional priorities

*Suggested strategies for improvement of
communication*

clearly defined guidelines, known to all
try NGT
let everyone know what you are doing – ask for their comments and
   (if possible) their support
work at good personal relationships
personal involvement
senior manager and other teachers to swap roles occasionally
ask colleagues to read/comment on report/findings
develop your ability to listen
allow for dialogue
allow colleagues to draw conclusions with you

buy a drink for anyone who will listen
be conscious of time constraints on others
plan for plenty of small group discussions
try to interest head in research
use a variety of methods of communication
be prepared to try again
plan for parents and governors to be educated about what really goes
  on in school
avoid jargon
be ever so humble

> *Attitudes of head and staff — suggested*
> *strategies*

go ahead without head's blessing
persuade head that school will derive kudos from project in eyes of
  HMIs, LEA, etc.
explain – enthuse – convince
institute a staff forum – staff draw up agenda and have a rotating
  chairperson or ask for rotating chairperson and rotating agenda at
  existing staff meetings
agree with validity of their point of view before pointing out the
  disadvantages
form links with other schools, so school isn't a closed community
manipulate positively
if you have participatory decision-making then implement decisions
be at the interview of new staff

(Elliott, 1982, 68–81)

The kinds of considerations invoked by these concerns are very different from those that first spring to mind when research tasks are approached conventionally. Here the question is not primarily one of maximizing research designs but of establishing enabling conditions. Consequently research is seen as interrelated with organization, curriculum and teaching: it has an educational as well as a research purpose. Indeed those things identified as constraints and problems often turn out to represent a hidden agenda for the research, being the real focus of attention rather than the topic, theme, or issue first identified. Perhaps this is part of the reason why those working in applied or action research tend to favour qualitative, or small-scale and exploratory quantitative techniques, not because of an ideological allegiance to certain philosophies of knowledge, but because such methods provide a flexibility in response that allows the focus of the research to move as the research progresses. The main problem with a complex survey design, or an elaborate experimental design, is that it fixes the focus, so categorizing constraints and problems as external factors or noise in the system. While more flexible designs carry the cost of a loss in precision, they have the advantage of being able to re-conceptualize the overall design to draw constraints and problems from the hidden curriculum onto centre-stage. This may indeed be the essential feature of 'responsiveness' in applied research, action research and evaluation.

The cumbersome nature of that last sentence prompts me to return to the issue of labels. I have deliberately used the terms 'applied research', 'action research' and even 'evaluation' as virtually interchangeable. I explained earlier that I was doing this in order to hold to a rather loose and generalized conception of what I took to be an identifiable approach to educational research, not wishing to be drawn too closely into fine distinctions between different approaches within that overall research direction. However, at this point it may clarify the discussion to indicate how these different labels might be used.

The central organizing idea is of a series of spiralling steps relating action and research. Drawing on ideas developed by Kurt Lewin, Stephen Kemmis (1981) represents this process diagrammatically (p. 196).

John Elliott (1981) has adapted this scheme further to allow for the kind of topical shift I described earlier. Elliott's diagrammatic representation of action research therefore builds an increased flexibility into the first and last stages of generating ideas and implementing changes (p. 197).

Ebbutt (1982) has pointed out that both these models lack any specification of dynamic or motive force that drives the models in practice. His own approach is to begin by looking at the kind of research people have actually done in order to classify it in terms of a series of labels. The diagram he produces is particularly useful as it helps to distinguish alternative strategies that might be taken in specific circumstances (pp. 198–9).

What this diagram does not include is the range of options open to the 'outside' researcher, except in the consultancy role included here, whereas the outlines sketched by Kemmis and

The action research spiral

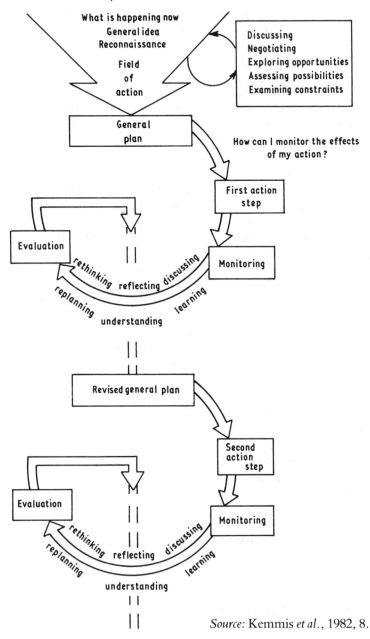

Source: Kemmis *et al.*, 1982, 8.

Action research as a spiral staircase

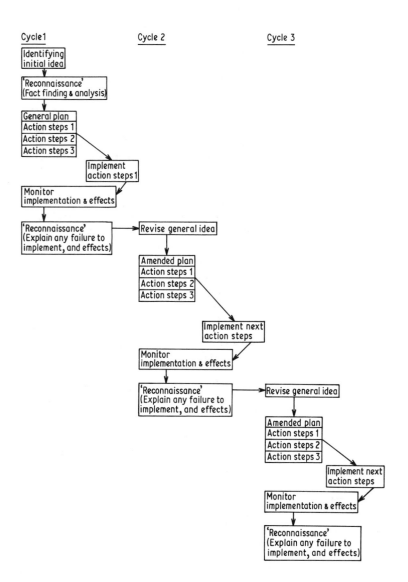

Source: Elliott, 1981, 3.

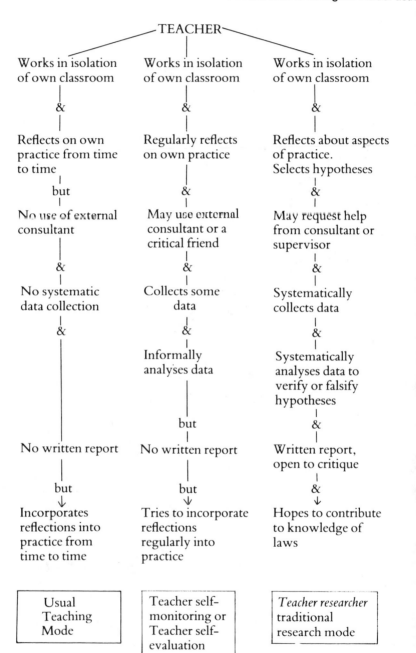

TEACHER

Works in isolation of own classroom	Works in isolation of own classroom	Works in isolation of own classroom
&	&	&
Reflects on own practice from time to time	Regularly reflects on own practice	Reflects about aspects of practice. Selects hypotheses
but	&	&
No use of external consultant	May use external consultant or a critical friend	May request help from consultant or supervisor
&	&	&
No systematic data collection	Collects some data	Systematically collects data
&	&	&
	Informally analyses data	Systematically analyses data to verify or falsify hypotheses
	but	&
No written report	No written report	Written report, open to critique
but	but	&
Incorporates reflections into practice from time to time	Tries to incorporate reflections regularly into practice	Hopes to contribute to knowledge of laws

| Usual Teaching Mode | Teacher self-monitoring or Teacher self-evaluation | *Teacher researcher* traditional research mode |

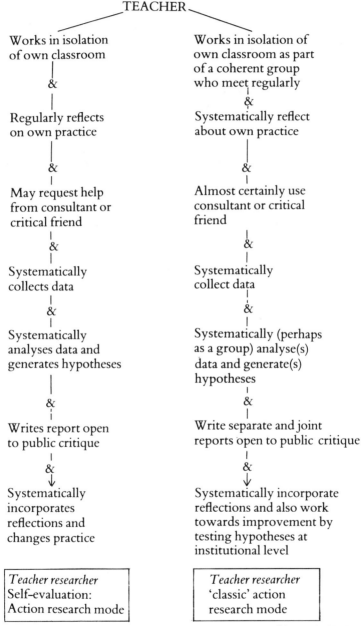

TEACHER

Works in isolation of own classroom	Works in isolation of own classroom as part of a coherent group who meet regularly
&	&
Regularly reflects on own practice	Systematically reflect about own practice
&	&
May request help from consultant or critical friend	Almost certainly use consultant or critical friend
&	&
Systematically collects data	Systematically collect data
&	&
Systematically analyses data and generates hypotheses	Systematically (perhaps as a group) analyse(s) data and generate(s) hypotheses
&	&
Writes report open to public critique	Write separate and joint reports open to public critique
&	&
Systematically incorporates reflections and changes practice	Systematically incorporate reflections and also work towards improvement by testing hypotheses at institutional level

Teacher researcher Self-evaluation: Action research mode	*Teacher researcher* 'classic' action research mode

Source: Ebbutt, 1982, 7.

Elliott may be generalized to outsider applications. Elsewhere Carr and Kemmis (1982) have provided a series of requirements which they argue need to be met more generally by educational science:

(a) it must reject positivist notions of rationality, objectivity and truth,

(b) it must employ the interpretive categories of teachers (or the other participants directly concerned with the practices under enquiry),

(c) it must provide ways of distinguishing ideas and interpretations which are systematically distorted by ideology from those which are not, and provide a view of how distorted self-understandings can be overcome,

(d) it must be concerned to identify and expose those aspects of the existing social order which frustrate rational change, and must be able to offer theoretical accounts which enable teachers (and other participants) to become aware of how they may be overcome, and

(e) it must be based on an explicit recognition that it is practical, in the sense that the question of its truth will be determined by the way it relates to practice.

(Carr and Kemmis, 1982, 136–7)

This book has been concerned with following through the implications of these requirements in practical terms, providing the basis for testing their feasibility and consequences.

In that sense, the book begins here, at the point where the reader becomes the active researcher.

References

Adelman, C. (n.d.) *Primary School. 'The Tins'*, Ford Teaching Project, Cambridge, Cambridge Institute of Education.

Adelman, C. (1976) *The Use of Objects in the Education of Children 3–5 Years*, Final Report HR3234/1, HR3061/1, London, SSRC.

Adelman, C. (1979) *Some Dilemmas of Institutional Evaluation and their Relationship to Preconditions and Procedures*, San Francisco, Calif., AERA.

Armstrong, M. (1981) *Closely Observed Children*, London, Writers and Readers.

Beasley, B. (1981) *The Reflexive Spectator in Classroom Research*, Adelaide, Australian Association for Research in Education.

Beasley, B. and Riordan, L. (1981) 'The classroom teacher as researcher', *English in Australia*, No. 55.

Bell, G. (1981) 'Action research networks', unpublished paper, Middlesbrough, Teesside Polytechnic.

Biddle, B. J. and Adams, R. S. (1971) *Realities of Teaching*, New York, Holt, Rinehart & Winston.

Blythe, R. (1972) *Akenfield*, Harmondsworth, Penguin.

Boehm, A. E., and Weinberg, R. A. (1977) *The Classroom Observer: A Guide for Developing Observation Skills*, New York, Teachers College Press.

Boehm, V. R. (1980) 'Research in the "Real World": a conceptual model', *Personnel Psychology*, 33, Autumn, 495–503.

Borg, W. R. and Gall, M. D. (1979) *Educational Research*, 3rd edn, New York, Longman.

Browning, L. *et al.* (n.d.) *Team Based Action Research*, Ford Teaching Project, Cambridge, Cambridge Institute of Education.

Cane, B. and Schroeder, C. (1970) *The Teacher and Research*, Slough, NFER.

Carr, W. and Kemmis, S. (1982) *Becoming Critical: Knowing through Action Research*, Geelong, Deakin University Press.

Chanan, G. and Delamont, S. (eds) (1975) *Frontiers of Classroom Research*, Slough, NFER.

Collier, J. (1967) *Visual Anthropology: Photography as a Research Method*, New York, Holt, Rinehart & Winston.

Cosgrove, S. (1981) *Using Action Research in the Classroom and the School: A Teacher's View*, Adelaide, Australian Association for Research in Education.

Dabbs, J. (1982) 'Making things visible', in van Maanen, J., Dabbs, J. and Faulkner, R. (eds), *Varieties of Qualitative Research*, Beverly Hills, Sage.

Delamont, S. (1983) *Interaction in the Classroom*, 2nd edn, London, Methuen.

Douglas, J. D. (ed.) (1972) *The Relevance of Sociology*, New York, Appleton–Century–Crofts.

Ebbutt, D. (1982) 'Educational Action Research: some general concerns and specific quibbles', mimeo, TIQL, Cambridge, Cambridge Institute of Education.

Elliott, J. (n.d.) *Three Points of View in the Classroom*, Ford Teaching Project, Cambridge, Cambridge Institute of Education.

Elliott, J. (1981) *Action Research: A Framework for Self Evaluation in Schools*, TIQL Working Paper No. 1, Cambridge, Cambridge Institute of Education.

Elliott, J. (1982) 'Action Research into action research', *Classroom Action Research Bulletin*, No. 5, Cambridge, Cambridge Institute of Education.

EPIE Information Unit (1972) *Early Childhood Programs*, tape-slide series, New York, EPIE Institute.

Erickson, F. and Wilson, J. (1982) *Sights and Sounds of Life in Schools*, Research Series No. 125, Ann Arbor, Mich., Institute for Research in Teaching, College of Education, University of Michigan.

Esterson, A. (1970) *The Leaves of Spring: Schizophrenia, Family and Sacrifice*, London, Tavistock.

Faulkner, R. (1982) 'Improvising on a triad', in van Maanen, J. *et al.*, *Varieties of Qualitative Research*, Beverly Hills, Calif., Sage, 65–102.

Fensham, P. *et al.* (1983) *Case Studies of School and the Transition to Work*, Report to ERDC (Canberra), London, Routledge & Kegan Paul.

Filstead, W. J. (ed.) (1970) *Qualitative Methodology*, Chicago, Markham.

Flanders, N. A. (1970) *Analyzing Teacher Behavior*, Reading, Mass., Addison-Wesley.

Forsyth, K. and Wood, J. (n.d.) 'Summary of classroom research techniques', in Elliott, J. and Adelman, C. (eds), *Ways of Doing*

Research in Your Own Classroom, Ford Teaching Project, Cambridge, Cambridge Institute of Education, 25–36.

Fox, G. T. (1978) *Residual Impact of the 1975 CMTI*. A Report prepared for Teacher Corps by the School of Education, University of Wisconsin, Madison.

Fox, G. T. *et al.* (1975) *Using Photographs for Interpretation*, Technical Report No. 4, Madison, Wisc., Teacher Corps, Corps Member Training Institution, University of Wisconsin.

Galton, M. (1978) *British Mirrors: A Collection of Classroom Observation Instruments*, Leicester, School of Education, University of Leicester.

Giroux, H. A. (1981) *Ideology, Culture and the Process of Schooling*, Brighton, Falmer Press.

Gray, P. J. *et al.* (1983) *A Guide Book for Conducting Field Trials of New Methods*, Report No. 77, Research on Evaluation Program, Portland, Ore., North Western Regional Educational Laboratory.

Hamilton, D. *et al.* (eds) (1977) *Beyond the Numbers Game*, London, Macmillan.

Hammersley, M. (1983) *Ethnography of Schooling*, Driffield, Nafferton.

Hammersley, M. and Atkinson, P. (1983) *Ethnography: Principles in Practice*, London, Tavistock.

Holly, M. L. (1984) *Keeping a Personal-professional Journal*, Geelong, Deakin University Press.

Hook, C. (1981) *Studying Classrooms*, Geelong, Deakin University Press.

Hull, C. (1983) 'Between the lines: the analysis of interview data as an exact art', mimeo, Norwich, Centre for Applied Research in Education, University of East Anglia.

Ireland, D. and Russell, T. (1978) 'Pattern analysis as used in the Ottawa Valley Teaching Project', *CARN Newsletter*, Cambridge, Cambridge Institute of Education, 21.

Johnson, K. (1980) *Timetabling*, London, Hutchinson.

Kaufman, B. (1964) *Up the Down Staircase*, Englewood Cliffs, NJ, Prentice-Hall.

Kemmis, S. and Robottom, I. (1981) 'Principles of procedure in curriculum evaluation', *Journal of Curriculum Studies*, 13 (2).

Kemmis, S. *et al.* (1982) *The Action Research Planner*, Geelong, Deakin University Press.

Kohl, H. (1968) *36 Children*, London, Gollancz.

Kounin, J. S. (1970) *Discipline and Group Management in Classrooms*, New York, Holt, Rinehart & Winston.

Lambert, R. and Millham, S. (1968) *The Hothouse Society*, London, Weidenfeld & Nicolson.

McCall, G. J. and Simmons, J. L. (eds) (1969) *Issues in Participant Observation*, Reading, Mass., Addison-Wesley.

MacDonald, B. and Kushner, S. (eds) (1983) *Bread and Dreams: A Case Study of Bilingual Schooling in the USA*, Norwich, Centre for Applied Research in Education, University of East Anglia.

MacDonald, B. and Sanger, J. (1982) 'Just for the record?: notes towards a theory of interviewing in evaluation', in House, E. (ed.), *Evaluation Review Studies Annual*, Beverly Hills, Sage, 7, 175–98.

MacDonald, B. and Stake, R. (1974) 'The first year of the National Development Programme in Computer-Assisted Learning from an issues perspective', unpublished evaluation report, Norwich, Centre for Applied Research in Education, University of East Anglia.

MacDonald, B. and Walker, R. (1974) *Information Evaluation Research and the Problem of Control*, SAFARI Working Paper No. 1, Norwich, Centre for Applied Research in Education, University of East Anglia.

MacPherson, A. (ed.) (October 1977 onwards) *Collaborative Research Newsletter*, Edinburgh, Centre for Educational Sociology, University of Edinburgh.

Millman, J. (1981) 'A checklist procedure', in Smith, N. L. (ed.), *New Techniques for Evaluation*, Beverly Hills, Sage.

Mitchell, N. and Fox, G. T. (1978) 'How music means in a Residual Impact Study', in Fox, G. T. *et al.*, *Residual Impact of the 1975 CMTI*, Madison, Wisc., University of Wisconsin, 163–72.

Nisbet, J. and Entwhistle, N. J. (1970) *Educational Research Methods*, London, University of London Press.

Nixon, J. (1981) *A Teachers' Guide to Action Research*, London, Grant McIntyre.

Parlett, M. and Hamilton, D. (1972) *Evaluation as Illumination*, Occasional Paper No. 9, Edinburgh, Centre for Research in Educational Sciences, University of Edinburgh.

Pick, C. and Walker, R. (1976) *Other Rooms, Other Voices*, radio script, Norwich, Centre for Applied Research in Education, University of East Anglia.

Popham, W. J. and Carlson, D. (1977) 'Deep, dark deficits of adversary evaluation', *Educational Researcher*, 6, 3–6.

Richardson, E. (1973) *The Teacher, the School and the Task of Management*, London, Heinemann Educational Books.

Rowland, S. (1979) 'Ability-matching: a critique', *Forum*, 21 (3), 82–6.

Rowland, S. (1981) 'How to intervene: clues from the work of a 10 year old', *Forum*, 23 (2), 33–5.

Rowland, S. (1982) 'Teachers studying classroom learning', *Education 3–13*, 10 (2), 30–5.

Rudduck, J. (1981) 'The effects of systematic induction courses for pupils on pupils' perceptions of innovation', Centre for Applied Research in Education, University of East Anglia, SSRC Final Report Grant No. HR6848/1.

Schatzman, L. and Strauss, A. L. (1973) *Field Research*, Englewood Cliffs, NJ, Prentice-Hall.

Scriven, M. and Roth, J. (1977) *Evaluation Thesaurus*, Point Reyes, Calif., Edge Press.

Sharp, R. and Green, A. G. (1975) *Education and Social Control*, London, Routledge & Kegan Paul.

Shoemaker, J. S. (1982) 'Television presentations', in Smith, N. L. (ed.), *Communication Strategies in Evaluation*, Beverly Hills, Calif., Sage.

Simon, A. and Boyer, G. (eds) (1970) *Mirrors for Behavior*, Philadelphia, Research for Better Schools.

Simons, H. (ed.) (1980) *Towards a Science of the Singular*, Occasional Publications No. 10, Norwich, Centre for Applied Research in Education, University of East Anglia.

Smith, M. L. (1975) 'Evaluation of an outward-bound program', unpublished report, Boulder, Colo., University of Colorado.

Smith, N. L. (ed.) (1981a) *Metaphors for Evaluation*, Beverly Hills, Sage.

Smith, N. L. (ed.) (1981b) *New Techniques for Evaluation*, Beverly Hills, Sage.

Stake, R. E. (1972) 'An approach to the evaluation of instructional programs (program portrayal *vs* analysis)', AERA Annual Meeting, Chicago, AERA.

Stake, R. E. (1976) *Evaluating Educational Programmes: The Need and the Response*, Paris, OECD.

Stake, R. E. and Easley, J. E. (1977) *Survey Findings*, Booklet 15, Case Studies in Science Education, Urbana, Ill., University of Illinois College of Education.

Stake, R. E. and Gjerde, C. (1974) 'An evaluation of TCITY, the Twin City Institute for Talented Youth 1971', in Kraft, R. *et al.* (eds), *Four Evaluation Examples: Anthropological, Economic, Narrative and Portrayal*, AERA Monograph Series on Curriculum Evaluation, Chicago, Ill., Rand McNally.

Stenhouse, L. A. (1975) *An Introduction to Curriculum Research and Development*, London, Heinemann.

Stenhouse, L. A. (ed.) (1978) *Curriculum Research and Development in Action*, London, Heinemann.

Stenhouse, L. A. (1980) 'What counts as research?', unpublished paper, Norwich, Centre for Applied Research in Education, University of East Anglia.

Stenhouse, L. A. (1983) *Authority, Education and Emancipation*, London, Heinemann.

Stinnett, T. M. (1957) 'Check that statistic!', *Educational Record*, 38, 83–90.

Stubbs, M. and Delamont, S. (1976) *Explorations in Classroom Observations*, Chichester, Wiley.

Templin, P. A. (1979) *Photography as an Evaluation Technique*, Monograph No. 32, Research on Evaluation Program, Portland, Ore., North Western Regional Educational Laboratory.

Templin, P. A. (1982) 'Still photography in evaluation', in Smith, N. L. (ed.), *Communication Strategies in Evaluation*, Beverly Hills, Calif., Sage.

Tripp, D. (1983a) 'Coauthorship and negotiation: the interview as an act of creation', paper first given to the annual conference of the Australian Association for Research in Education (Adelaide 1981), mimeo, Murdoch University.

Tripp, D. (1983b) 'Greenhill: a Western Australian case study', in Fensham, P. *et al.*, *Case Studies of School and the Transition to Work*, Report to ERDC (Canberra), London, Routledge & Kegan Paul.

Tukey, J. W. (1977) *Exploratory Data Analysis*, Reading, Mass., Addison-Wesley.

Wagner, J. (ed.) (1979) *Images of Information: Still Photography in the Social Sciences*, Beverly Hills, Calif., Sage.

Walker, R. (1974) 'The Nuffield approach', unpublished paper, Norwich, Centre for Applied Research in Education, University of East Anglia.

Walker, R. (1982) *The Observational Work of LEA Inspectors and Advisers*, Norwich, Centre for Applied Research in Education, University of East Anglia.

Webb, E. J., Campbell, D. T., Schwartz, R. D. and Sechrest, L. (1966) *Unobtrusive Measures: Non-reactive Research in the Social Sciences*, Chicago, Rand McNally.

Willis, P. (1977) *Learning to Labour*, Farnborough, Saxon House.

Wolf, R. L. (1975) 'Trial by jury: a new evaluation method. 1. The process', *Phi Delta Kappa*, 185–7.

Woods, P. (1979) *The Divided School*, London, Routledge & Kegan Paul.

Woods, P. (ed.) (1980a) *Pupil Strategies*, London, Croom Helm.

Woods, P. (1980b) *Teacher Strategies*, London, Croom Helm.
Woods, P. and Hammersley, M. (1976) *School Experience*, London, Croom Helm.

Author index

Subject index